Rebuses for Readers

REBUSES FOR READERS

Pat Martin
Joanne Kelly
Kay Grabow

Illustrated by Pat Martin

1992
TEACHER IDEAS PRESS
A division of
Libraries Unlimited, Inc.
Englewood, Colorado

for our families

TEACHER IDEAS PRESS
A Division of
Libraries Unlimited, Inc.
P.O. Box 6633
Englewood, CO 80155-6633

Library of Congress Cataloging-in-Publication Data

Martin, Pat, 1937-
    Rebuses for readers / Pat Martin, Joanne Kelly, Kay Grabow ; illustrated by Pat Martin.
        ix, 138 p. 22x28 cm.
    Includes bibliographical references and index.
    ISBN 0-87287-920-8
    1. Riddles, Juvenile. 2. Rebuses. 3. Picture puzzles.
I. Kelly, Joanne. II. Grabow, Kay. III. Title.
PN6371.5.M365 1992
398.6--dc20   92-5014
                                                        CIP

P

Contents

Introduction

Children of all ages are fascinated by rebus puzzles. Display one on an overhead projector or a bulletin board and watch the children focus on it intently, the lips soundlessly forming and reforming words until the happy smiles when recognition dawns. Then comes the inevitable reaction, "Do another one!"

How to Solve a Rebus

Picture writing is an ancient art. The Egyptians began recording their own histories in neat rows of picture symbols. During the nineteenth century the rebus was often used in children's books. Whole books, in fact, were produced in picture-writing format. Children today enjoy decoding the puzzle in figure 1 based on a verse from *Mother Goose in Hieroglyphics*, published by George Appleton, Philadelphia, in 1849, or the rebus stories found in *Picture Stories* by Miss Colquhoun, published by James Taylor, Edinburgh, in 1864.

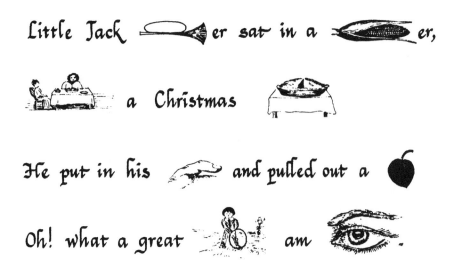

Fig. 1. Rebus based on verse from *Mother Goose in Hieroglyphics*. (Courtesy of the Lilly Library, Indiana University, Bloomington, Indiana.)

There are certain problem-solving techniques that can make these puzzles more fun and ensure a higher degree of success.

1. Rebus puzzles can be based on spelling or on sounds.

    T + 🍎 - ple   (T + Apple - ple) = TAP

    This rebus is based on spelling.

    T + 🍎 - L   (T + Apple - sound of L) = TAP

    This rebus is based on sound. (Both types of puzzles are used in this book.)

Advise children to sound out a word or phrase. If a plus or minus sign is linked to the word, they can begin by writing down the word they have deciphered, adding or subtracting the linked letter or sound. (This written step is needed only when solutions are not immediately apparent.) Children are quick to learn those techniques and continue to apply them independently.

2. Rebus solutions can be made easier through the forms of presentation. For example, younger children may need structure in order to recognize word groups. Draw a box around the letters and pictures that make up one word (see figure 2).

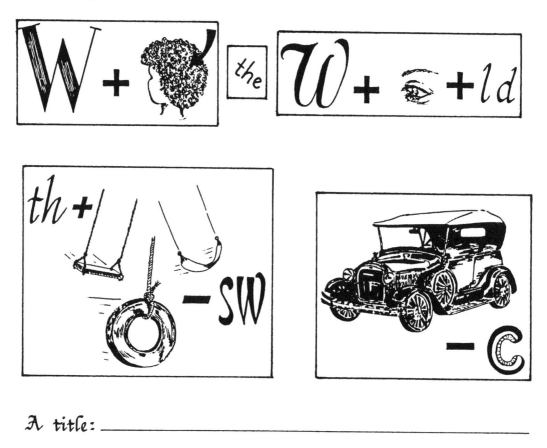

A title: _____

Fig. 2. Clues to the number of words using boxed pictures.

Another way to present a clue is to indicate the number of words on a working line beneath the puzzle. Draw lines for the number of letters in each word (see figure 3).

3. When introducing rebuses, begin with a group activity using a rebus based on a book title well known to most of the children. Make the rebus large enough for everyone to see at once, for example, on a bulletin board, flannel board, or overhead projector. Let the children discover the answer as a group, sounding out the words aloud. Thinking out loud stimulates enthusiasm and provides the uninitiated with clues about the process of solving the puzzles. Once someone has discovered the answer, go through the rebus step by step, writing down the words as they are sounded and spelled out. Remind the students that the answer may not always be correctly spelled. (Correct spellings are found in the bibliography.) Repeat this procedure a few more times until everyone has the idea.

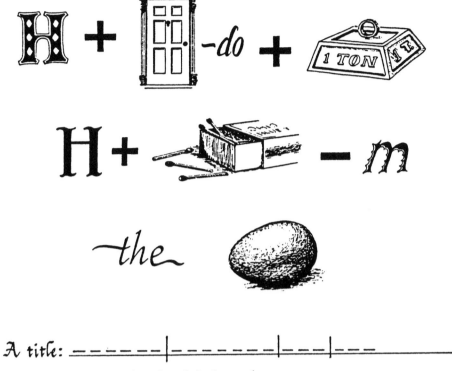

A title: $-----$ | $-------$ | $---$ | $---$

Fig. 3. Clues to the number of words in the puzzle.

How to Use *Rebuses for Readers*

Distribute copies of the puzzles to children to work on individually or in teams. Either staple the rebuses together into packets or hand them out one at a time. The rebuses can be used to reinforce the terms *setting* and *character* or to promote recognition of well-known authors and titles.

The rebuses can be used in several game formats. Use the overhead projector for a quiz bowl competition between teams. In constructing a board game, students might create several spaces that require a player to solve a rebus in order to move forward. Rebuses may be reduced in size and glued to index cards to create a matching card game in which some cards have rebuses and others have the solutions.

Extend learning opportunities by challenging students to create their own puzzles. Begin with those presented in chapter 5. Children select from the given puzzle parts and arrange their selections to form titles, authors, characters, or settings. There are numerous combinations that may be constructed to give the answer. Ask them to see how many they can discover. Also, teachers may want to give students the first symbol or two of a rebus and ask them to create the rest. Many answers are possible!

Encourage students to take the next step, creating their own rebuses based on their favorite books, authors, characters, and settings. They might use any of the puzzle parts in chapter 6, picking and choosing from the variety of clues, or they might create their own clues by clipping pictures from magazines and newspapers or even drawing some. Student-created puzzles can be copied and distributed or used as displays.

Students may enjoy putting together a class rebus book that contains rebuses created by teachers and students with blank pages for additional rebuses. The book could be checked out to share with families.

The puzzles in each chapter of *Rebuses for Readers* are arranged by the age of the intended audience of the book being depicted. This is not meant to restrict the use of the rebus to that age group. For example, sixth graders may enjoy deciphering an old friend such as *Curious George*, and precocious second graders, given a clue or two, may readily recognize *Pippi Longstocking*.

We hope your students enjoy solving rebuses as much as ours have. They not only stimulate interest in books but also promote problem solving and cooperative learning.

1
Fifty Titles in Rebus Form

Answers to Rebuses

For the Primary Grades

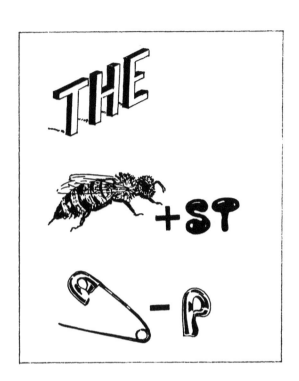

For the Intermediate Grades

For the Upper Grades

Clues for Chapter 1

Use the following clues to make rebuses easier for younger children. Give the clue verbally after the students have worked on a rebus for a few minutes. If children generally have difficulty with rebuses, write the clue on the original rebus before reproducing it. For every title there are two clues. The first clue is about the story itself and the second refers to a word or words contained in the title.

The Beast in Mrs. Rooney's Room
1. A second-grade boy
2. A teacher's name

Blueberries for Sal
1. A girl meets a bear.
2. The name of a fruit

Chicken Soup with Rice
1. It's delicious all year.
2. The name of a healthy food

Corduroy
1. A teddy bear
2. A type of cloth

Curious George
1. Monkey fun
2. A man's name

Frog and Toad Are Friends
1. Animal pals
2. The names of two types of pond creatures

Harold and the Purple Crayon
1. A little artist
2. Something used to draw pictures is in the title.

Horton Hatches the Egg
1. A patient elephant
2. A food that's easily cracked

Jumanji
1. A wild game
2. A name with two Js

Little Red Hiding Hood
1. An animal in disguise
2. A primary color

Millions of Cats
1. Too many pets
2. A large number

Miss Nelson Is Missing
1. A good teacher
2. A word that means *lost*

The Polar Express
1. A special train
2. A word sometimes used with bear

Strega Nona
1. A pasta-maker
2. Italian words

Where the Wild Things Are
1. Where monsters live
2. A word that means *not tame*

The BFG
1. A kind giant
2. Someone's initials are in the title.

The Best Christmas Pageant Ever	1.	A holiday program
	2.	The name of a holiday
The Boxcar Children	1.	Kids on their own
	2.	Something that carries freight
Bridge to Terabithia	1.	Tragic loss of a friend
	2.	The name of an imaginary kingdom
Bunnicula	1.	An unusual pet
	2.	A name made up of two words is in the title.
The Cricket in Times Square	1.	A talented insect
	2.	A place in New York City
Harry's Mad	1.	A know-it-all bird
	2.	A word that means *angry*
Henry Huggins	1.	An ordinary boy and his friends
	2.	The first and last name of a boy
Homer Price	1.	A boy's adventures
	2.	The title contains a word that means *cost*.
How to Eat Fried Worms	1.	An unusual bet
	2.	Squirmy animals are in the title.
The Indian in the Cupboard	1.	Tiny figures come to life.
	2.	A Native American is in the title.
The Lion, the Witch, and the Wardrobe	1.	A fantasy land
	2.	A place to store clothes
Little House on the Prairie	1.	A pioneer story
	2.	A small building
Misty of Chincoteague	1.	A pony story
	2.	The title contains a word that means *a bit rainy*.
Mr. Popper's Penguins	1.	Cool pets
	2.	A kind of bird
The Not-Just-Anybody Family	1.	Weird relatives
	2.	A word that means *relatives*
Pippi Longstocking	1.	Adventures of a funny girl
	2.	Something that can be worn is in the title.
Runaway Ralph	1.	A mouse on the move
	2.	Someone who leaves home is in the title.
Sounder	1.	A faithful dog
	2.	Part of the title is a noise.
Soup and Me	1.	Two mischievous friends
	2.	A hot food

The View from the Cherry Tree	1.	A boy sees a murder.
	2.	A fruit
Where the Sidewalk Ends	1.	Funny poems
	2.	A *concrete path* is in the title.
The Black Stallion	1.	A boy and a fast horse
	2.	A dark color
Cracker Jackson	1.	A boy rescuer
	2.	A crunchy food
A Gathering of Days	1.	A diary
	2.	A word that means the opposite of *nights*
The Great Brain	1.	A clever boy
	2.	The contents of the head
Homecoming	1.	Four on their own
	2.	Part of the title is a place where people live.
The Incredible Journey	1.	Three wilderness travelers
	2.	A trip
Little Women	1.	Four sisters
	2.	A word that means *females*
Rip Van Winkle	1.	A sleeper
	2.	The name of a vehicle
Roll of Thunder, Hear My Cry	1.	A poor family in the South
	2.	A noise is in the title.
The Secret Garden	1.	A hidden place
	2.	A place where flowers grow
Wait Till Helen Comes	1.	A spooky girl
	2.	A girl's name
Where the Red Fern Grows	1.	A boy and his hunting dogs
	2.	A plant
A Wrinkle in Time	1.	A supernatural search
	2.	A word that means *crease* is in the title.

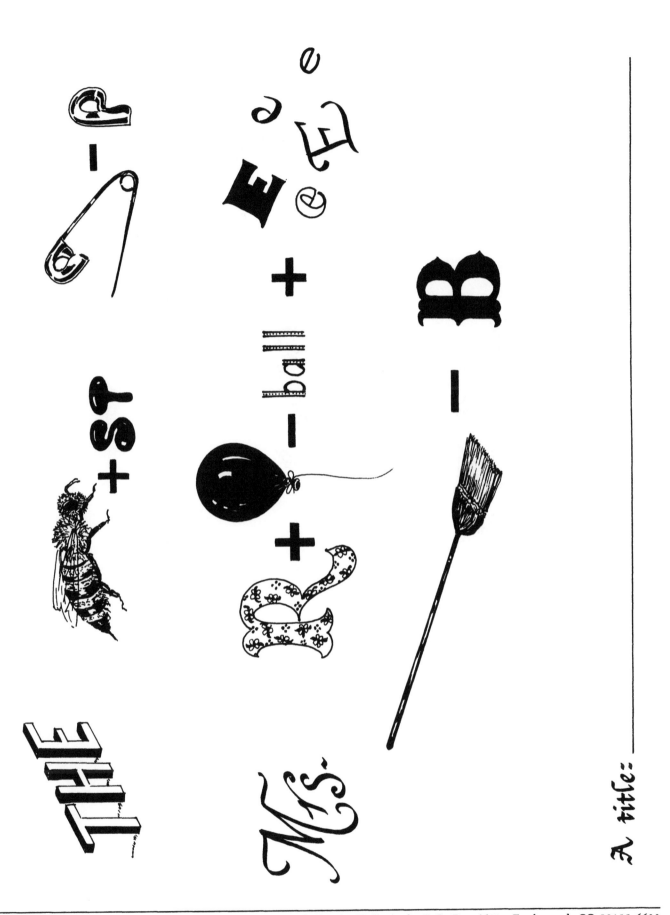

A title: _____

Rebuses for Readers. 1992. Teacher Ideas Press, a division of Libraries Unlimited • P.O. Box 6633 • Englewood, CO 80155-6633

5

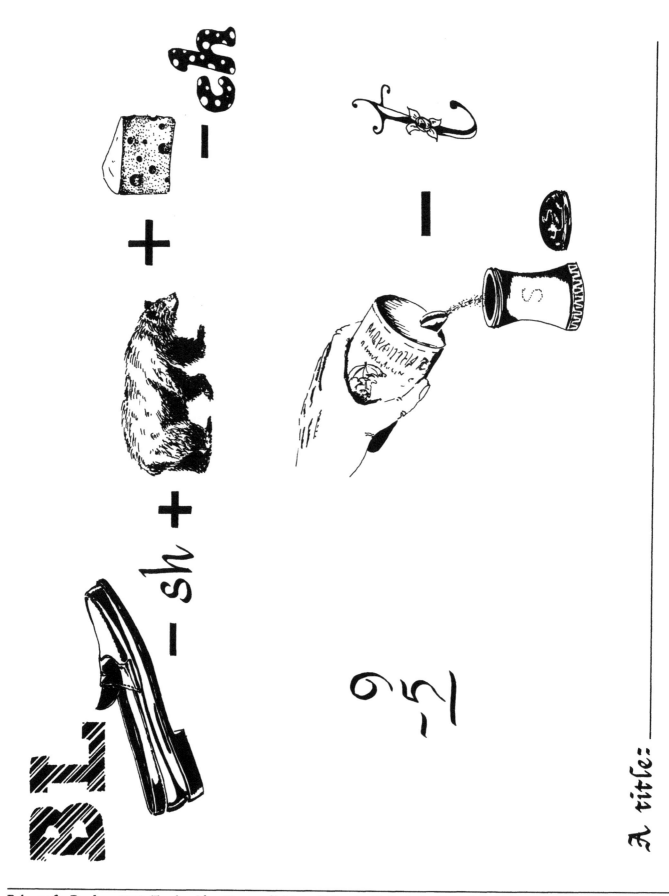

A title: _____

Rebuses for Readers. 1992. Teacher Ideas Press, a division of Libraries Unlimited • P.O. Box 6633 • Englewood, CO 80155-6633

6

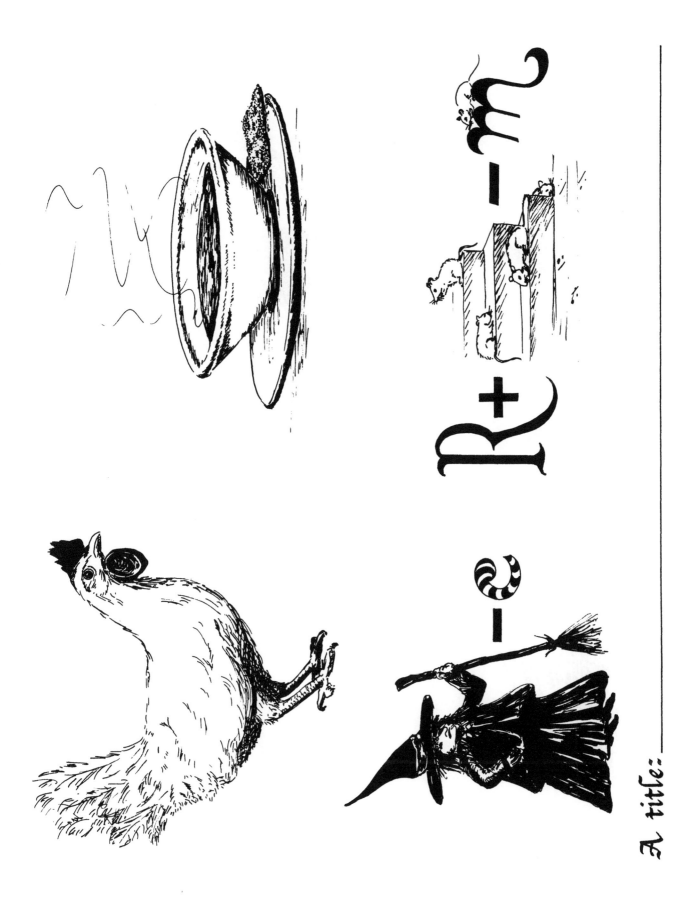

A title: _____

Rebuses for Readers. 1992. Teacher Ideas Press, a division of Libraries Unlimited • P.O. Box 6633 • Englewood, CO 80155-6633

7

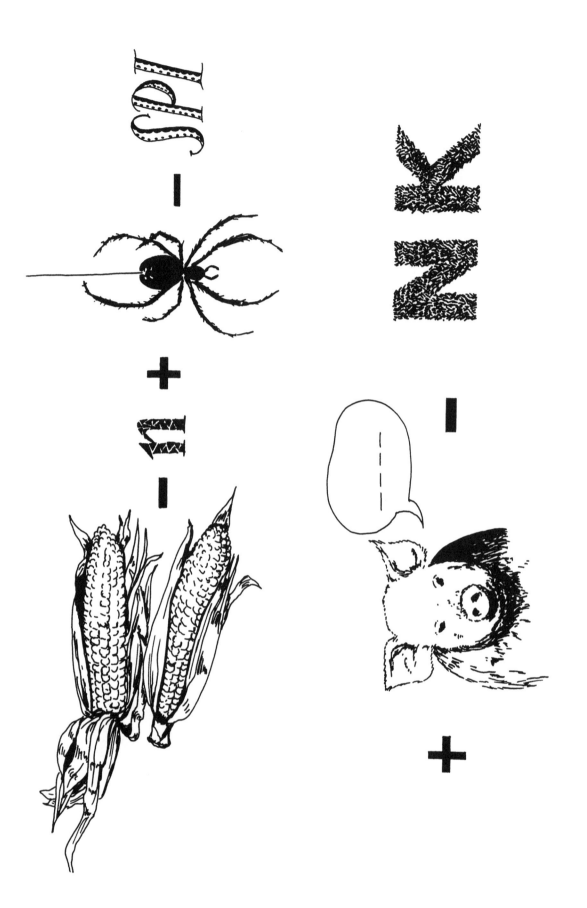

A title: _____

Rebuses for Readers. 1992. Teacher Ideas Press, a division of Libraries Unlimited • P.O. Box 6633 • Englewood, CO 80155-6633

8

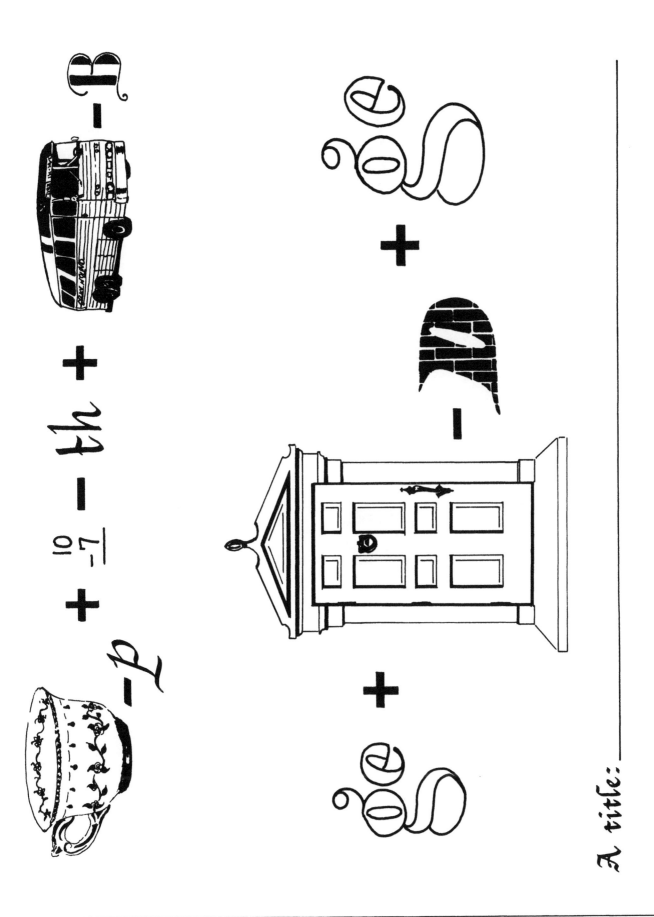

A title: _____

Rebuses for Readers. 1992. Teacher Ideas Press, a division of Libraries Unlimited • P.O. Box 6633 • Englewood, CO 80155-6633

9

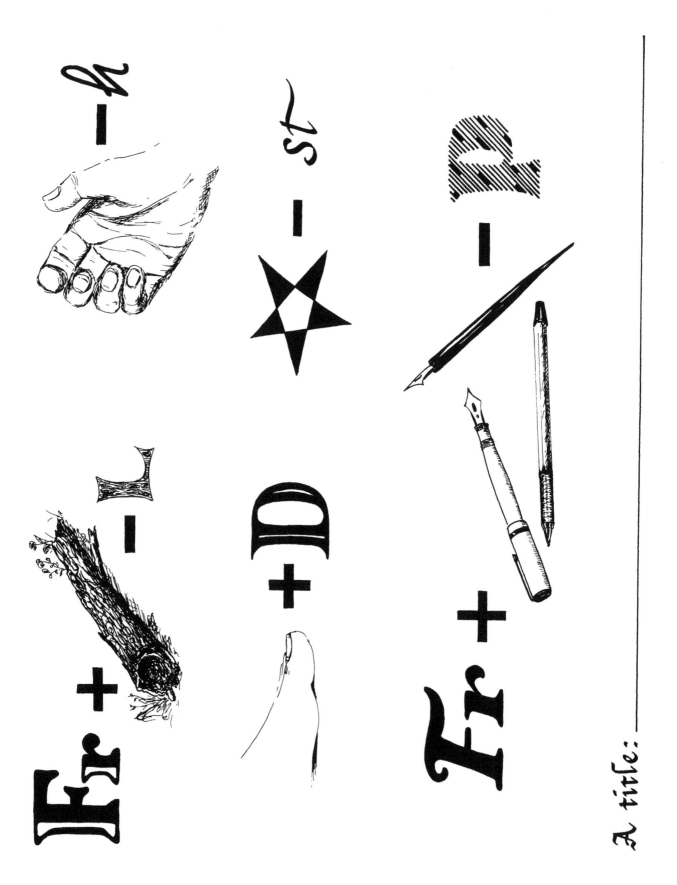

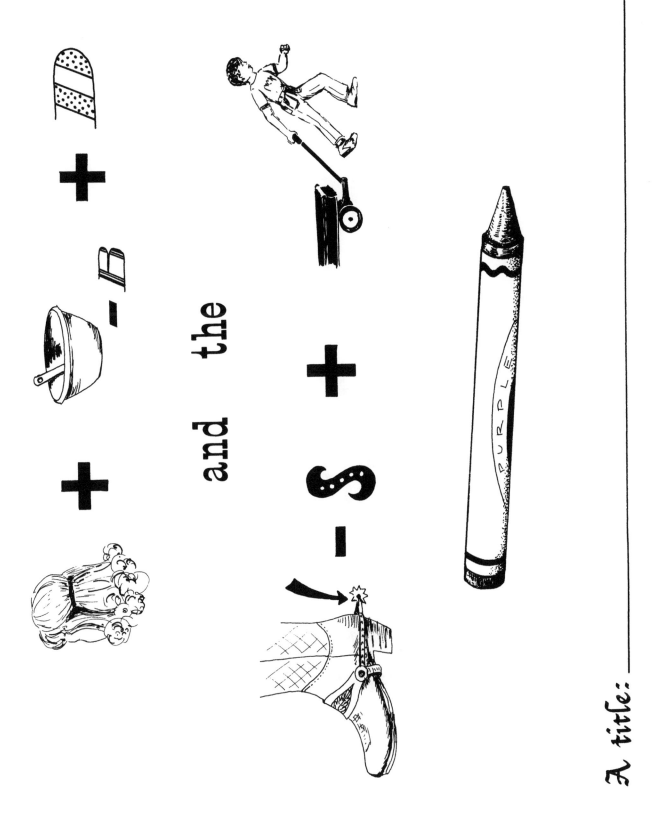

A title: _____

Rebuses for Readers. 1992. Teacher Ideas Press, a division of Libraries Unlimited • P.O. Box 6633 • Englewood, CO 80155-6633

11

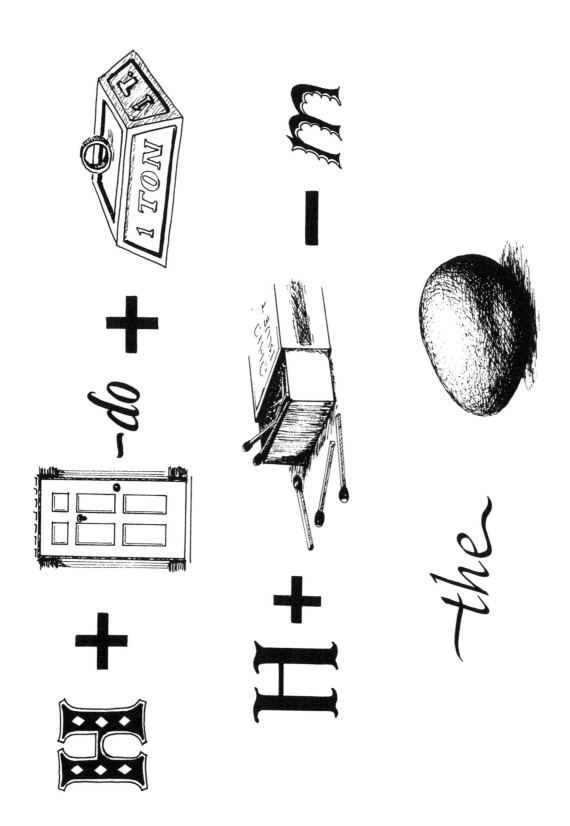

Rebuses for Readers. 1992. Teacher Ideas Press, a division of Libraries Unlimited • P.O. Box 6633 • Englewood, CO 80155-6633

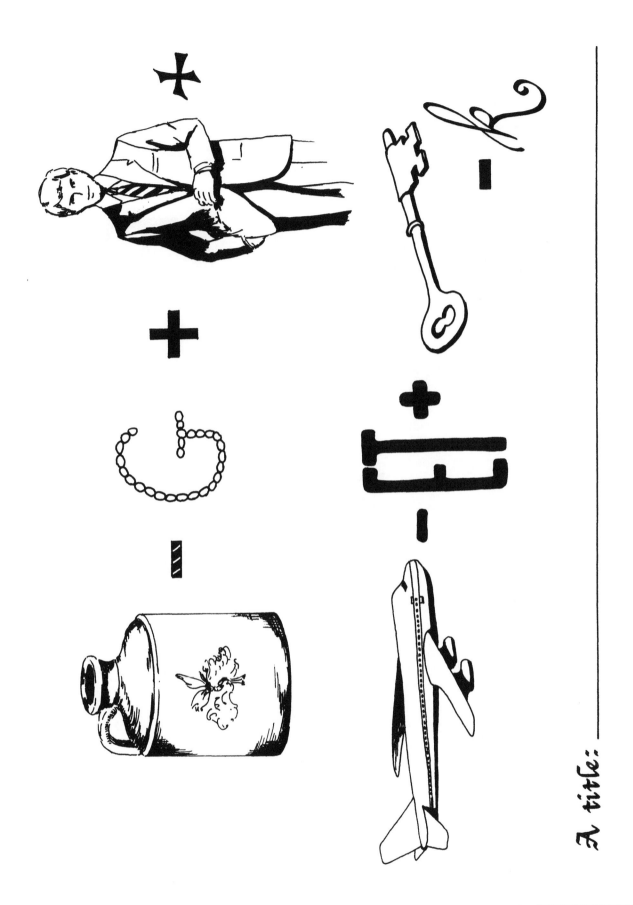

Rebuses for Readers. 1992. Teacher Ideas Press, a division of Libraries Unlimited • P.O. Box 6633 • Englewood, CO 80155-6633

13

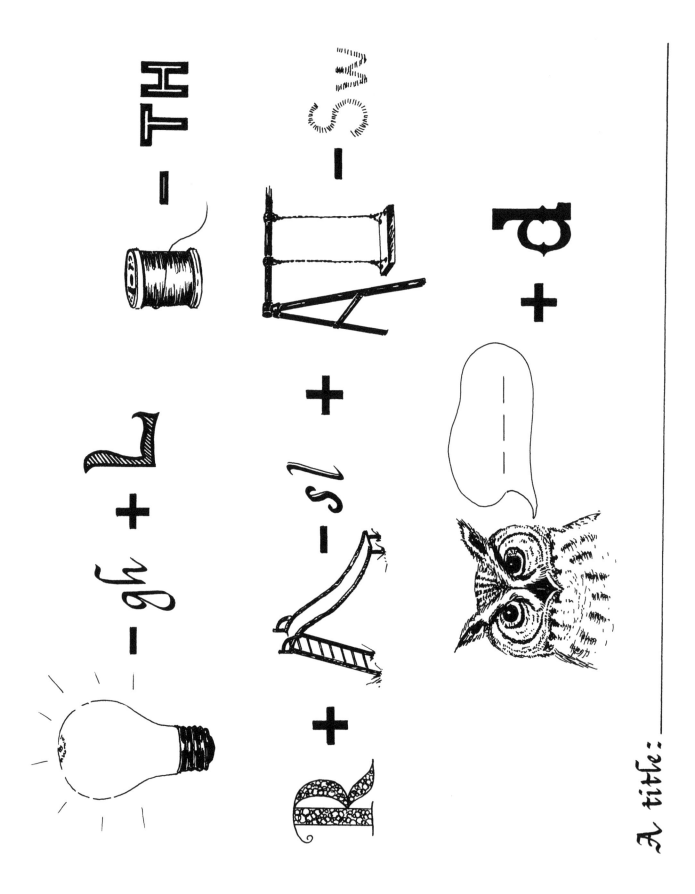

Rebuses for Readers. 1992. Teacher Ideas Press, a division of Libraries Unlimited • P.O. Box 6633 • Englewood, CO 80155-6633

14

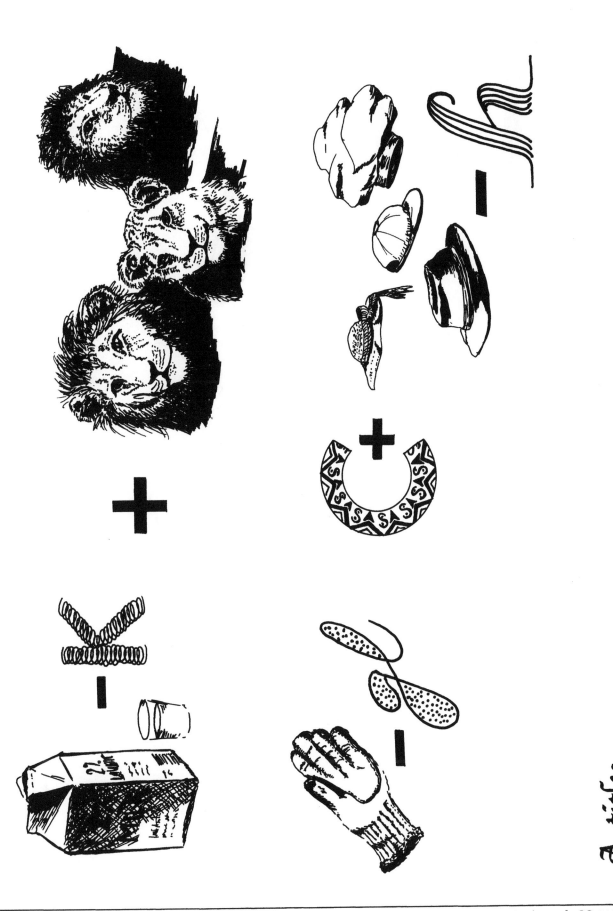

Rebuses for Readers. 1992. Teacher Ideas Press, a division of Libraries Unlimited • P.O. Box 6633 • Englewood, CO 80155-6633

15

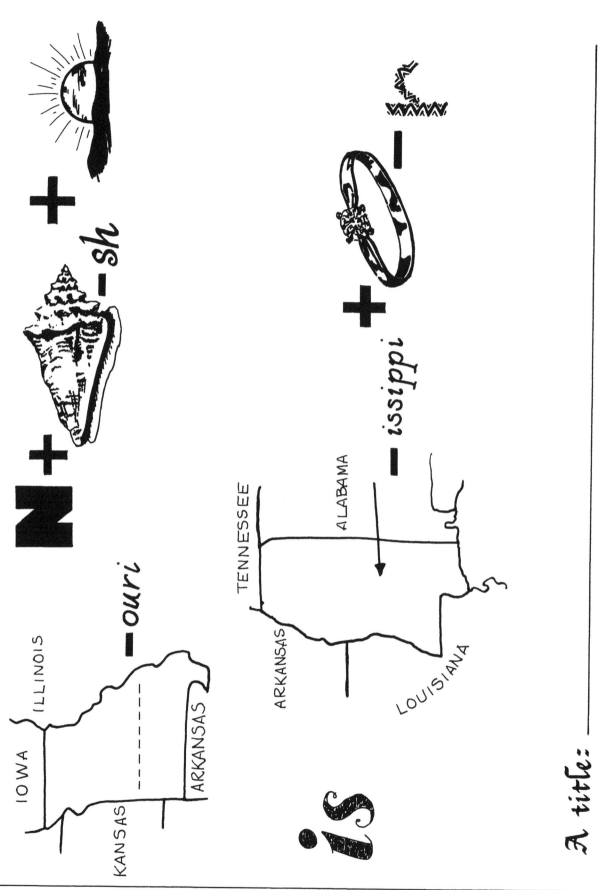

A title: _____

Rebuses for Readers. 1992. Teacher Ideas Press, a division of Libraries Unlimited • P.O. Box 6633 • Englewood, CO 80155-6633

16

A title: _____

Rebuses for Readers. 1992. Teacher Ideas Press, a division of Libraries Unlimited • P.O. Box 6633 • Englewood, CO 80155-6633

17

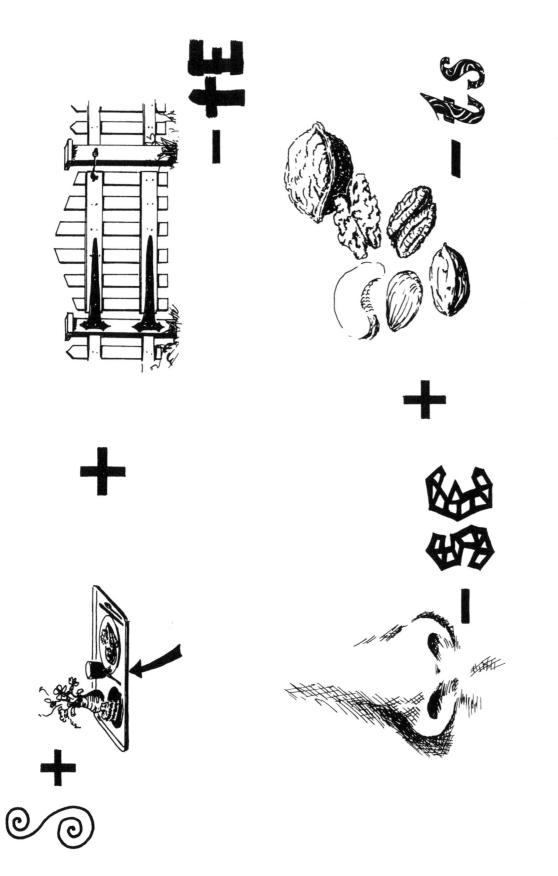

Rebuses for Readers. 1992. Teacher Ideas Press, a division of Libraries Unlimited • P.O. Box 6633 • Englewood, CO 80155-6633

18

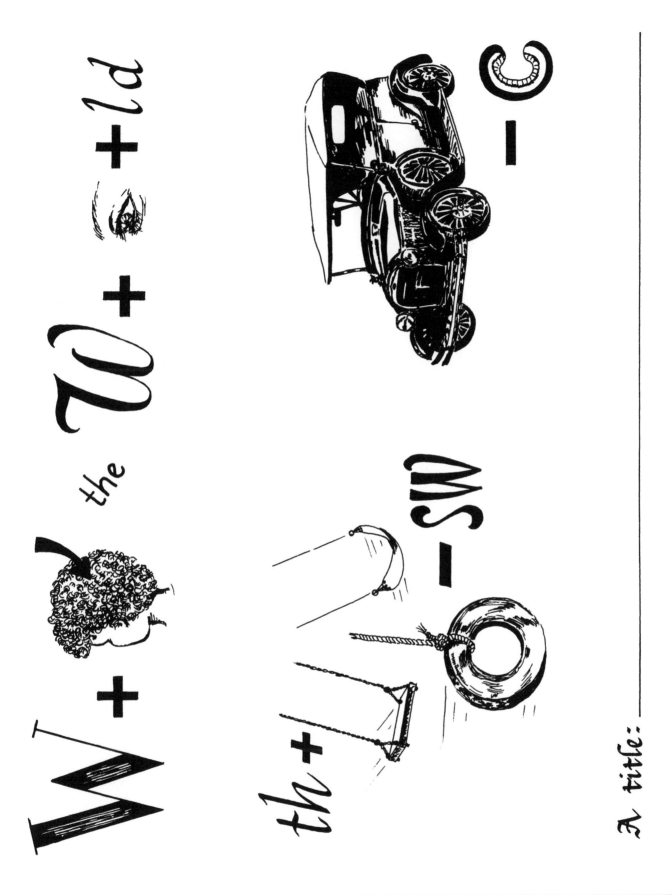

A title: _____

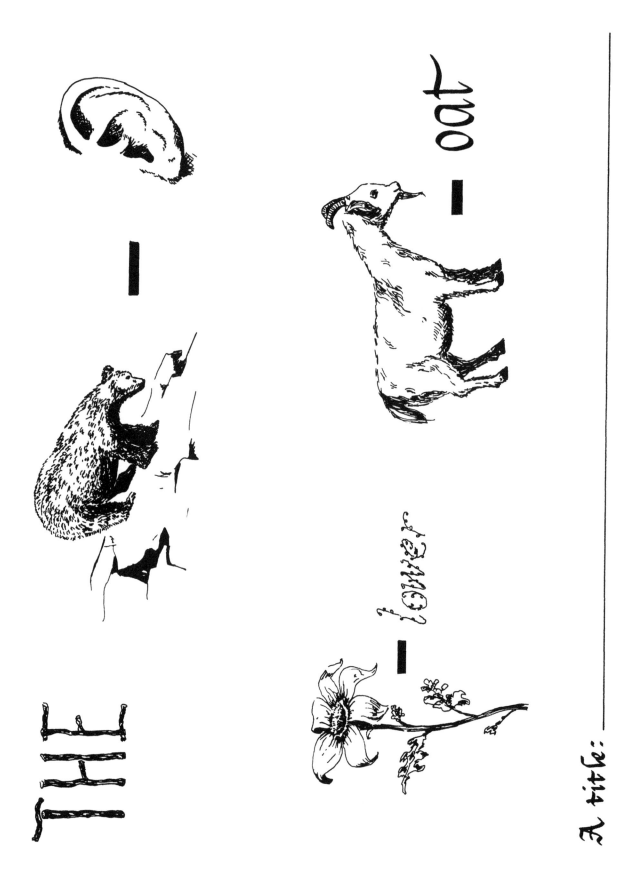

A title: _____

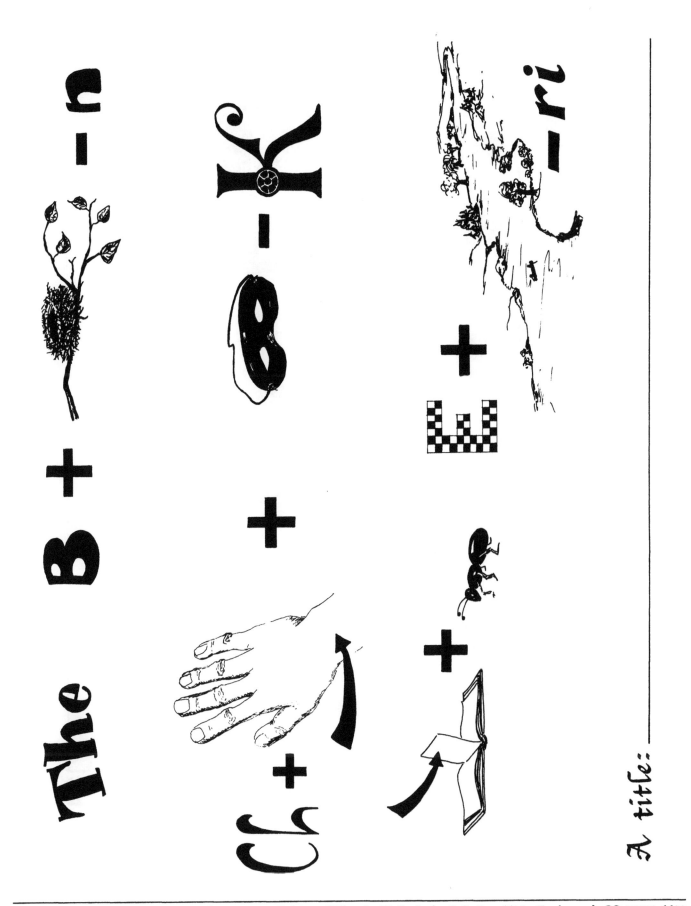

Rebuses for Readers. 1992. Teacher Ideas Press, a division of Libraries Unlimited • P.O. Box 6633 • Englewood, CO 80155-6633

21

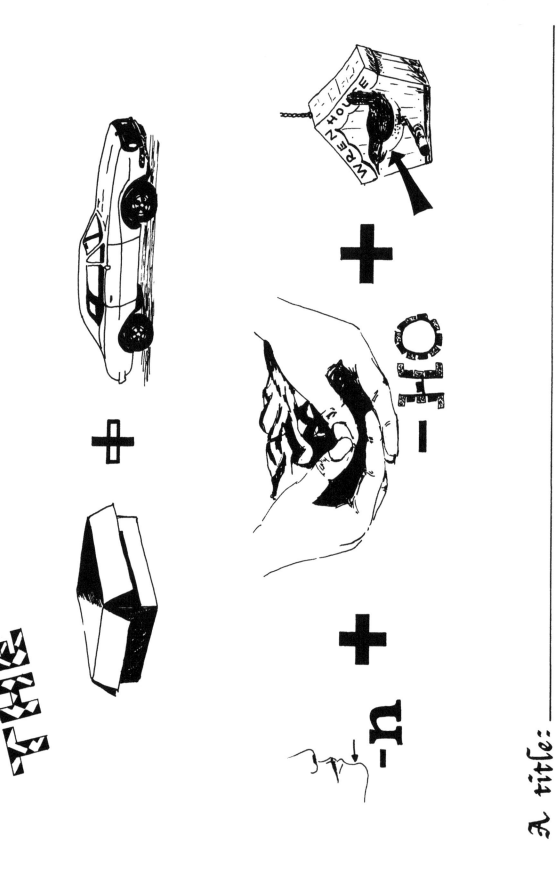

A title: _____

22

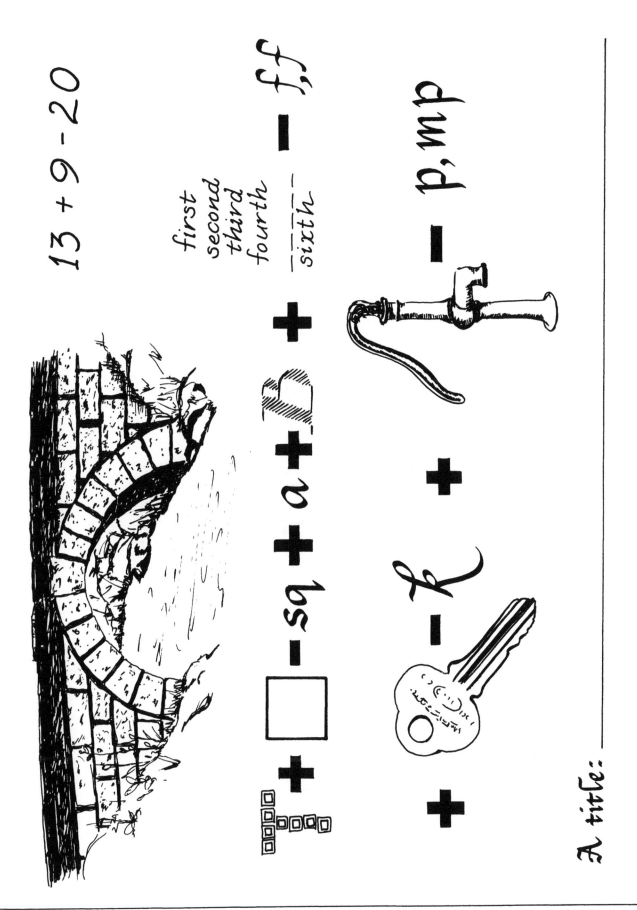

13 + 9 - 20

first
second
third
fourth
—
sixth

ff

− sq + a +

+

+

p, mp

− k

+

A title: _____

Rebuses for Readers. 1992. Teacher Ideas Press, a division of Libraries Unlimited • P.O. Box 6633 • Englewood, CO 80155-6633

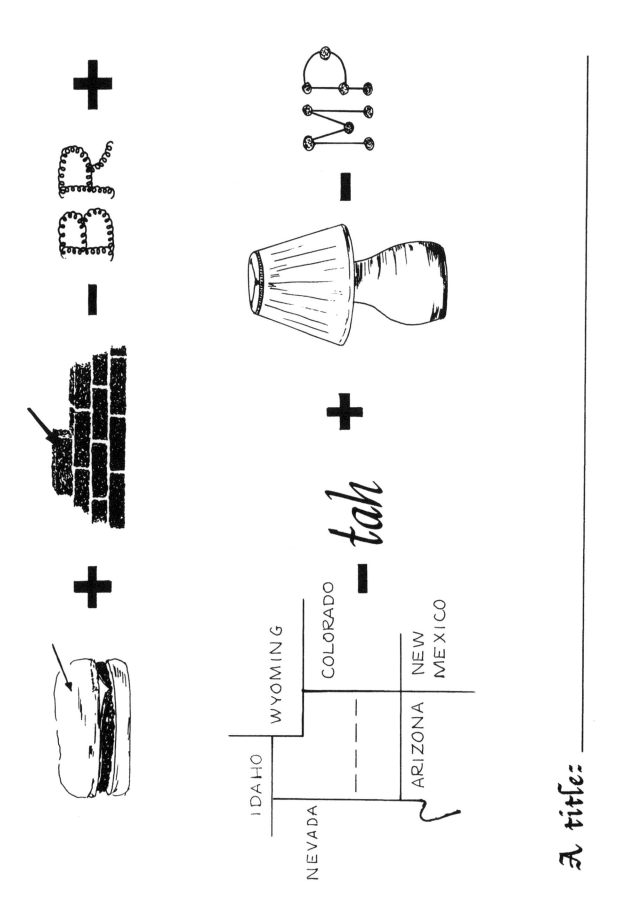

A title: _____

Rebuses for Readers. 1992. Teacher Ideas Press, a division of Libraries Unlimited • P.O. Box 6633 • Englewood, CO 80155-6633

24

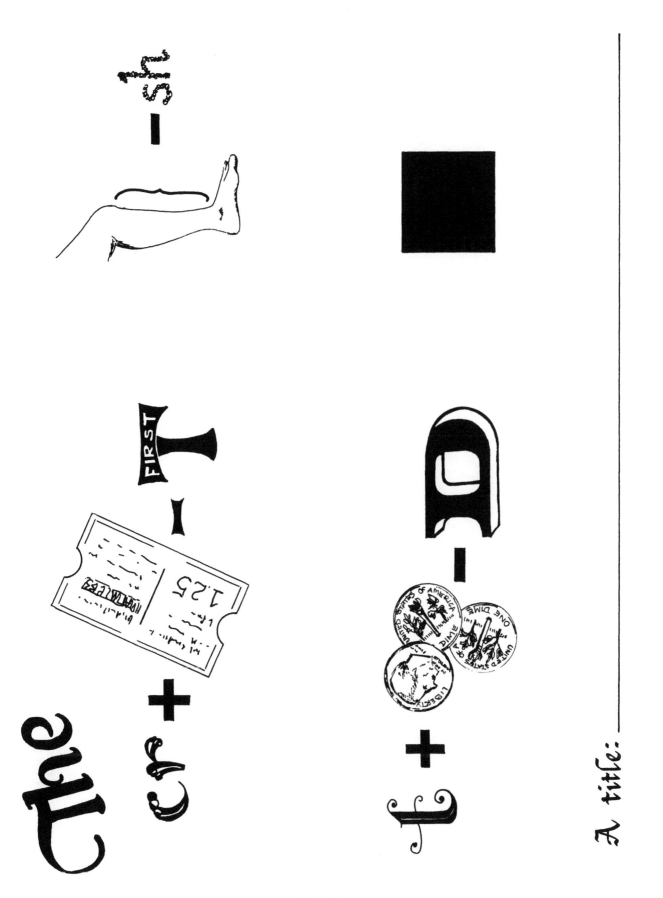

Rebuses for Readers. 1992. Teacher Ideas Press, a division of Libraries Unlimited • P.O. Box 6633 • Englewood, CO 80155-6633

25

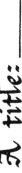

A title: _____

Rebuses for Readers. 1992. Teacher Ideas Press, a division of Libraries Unlimited • P.O. Box 6633 • Englewood, CO 80155-6633

26

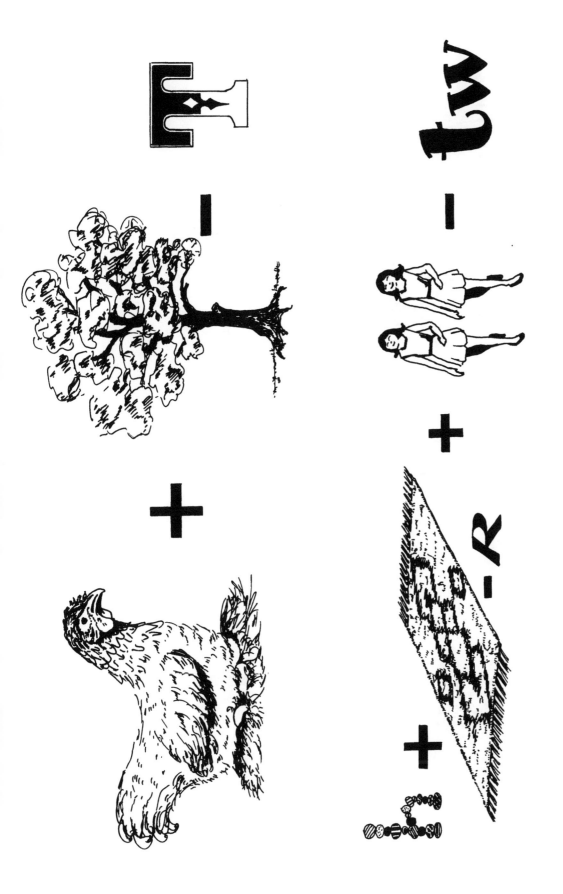

A title: _____

Rebuses for Readers. 1992. Teacher Ideas Press, a division of Libraries Unlimited • P.O. Box 6633 • Englewood, CO 80155-6633

27

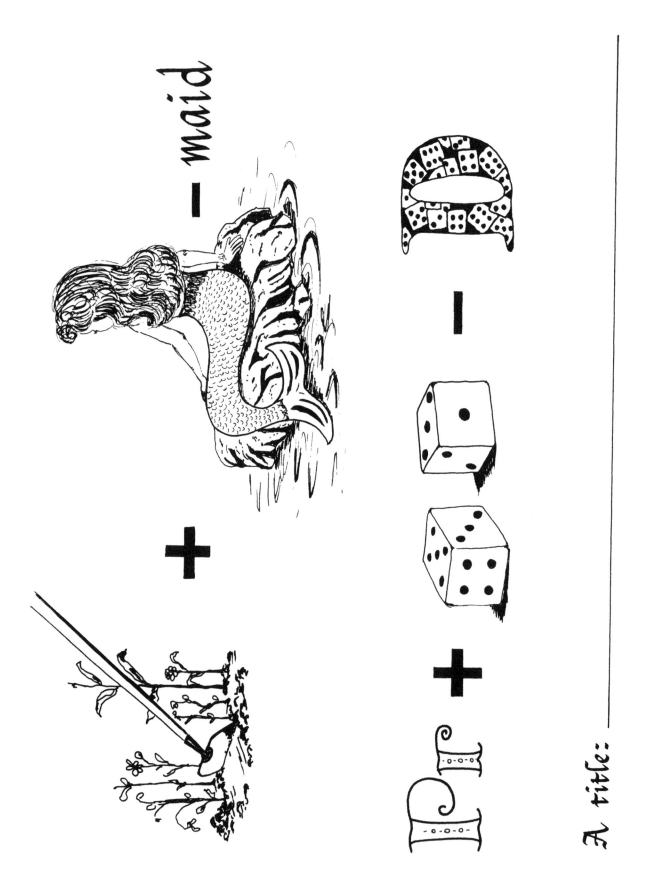

− maid

+

−

+

A title: _____

Rebuses for Readers. 1992. Teacher Ideas Press, a division of Libraries Unlimited • P.O. Box 6633 • Englewood, CO 80155-6633

28

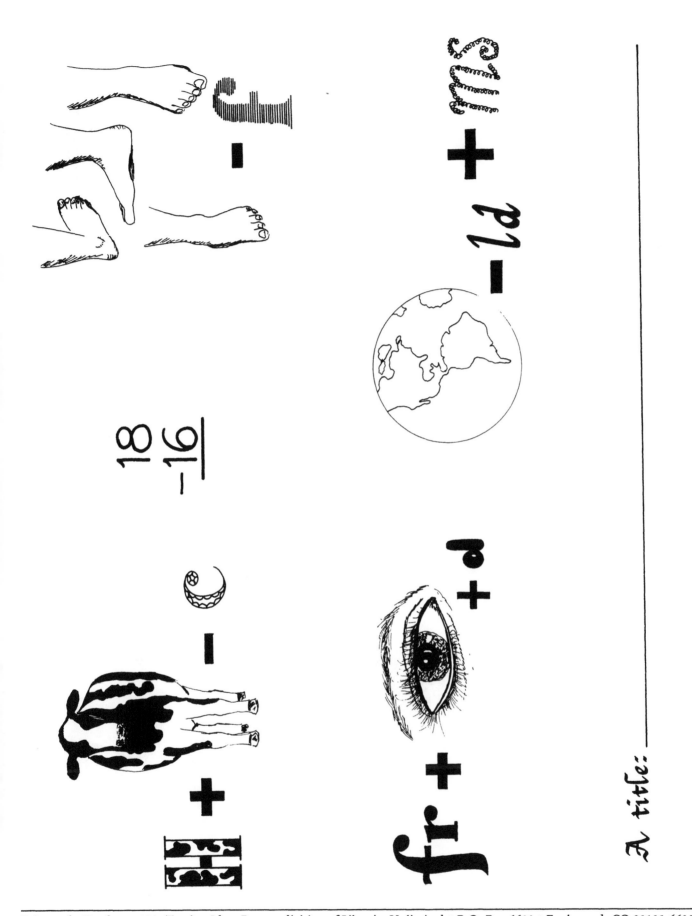

A title: _____

Rebuses for Readers. 1992. Teacher Ideas Press, a division of Libraries Unlimited • P.O. Box 6633 • Englewood, CO 80155-6633

29

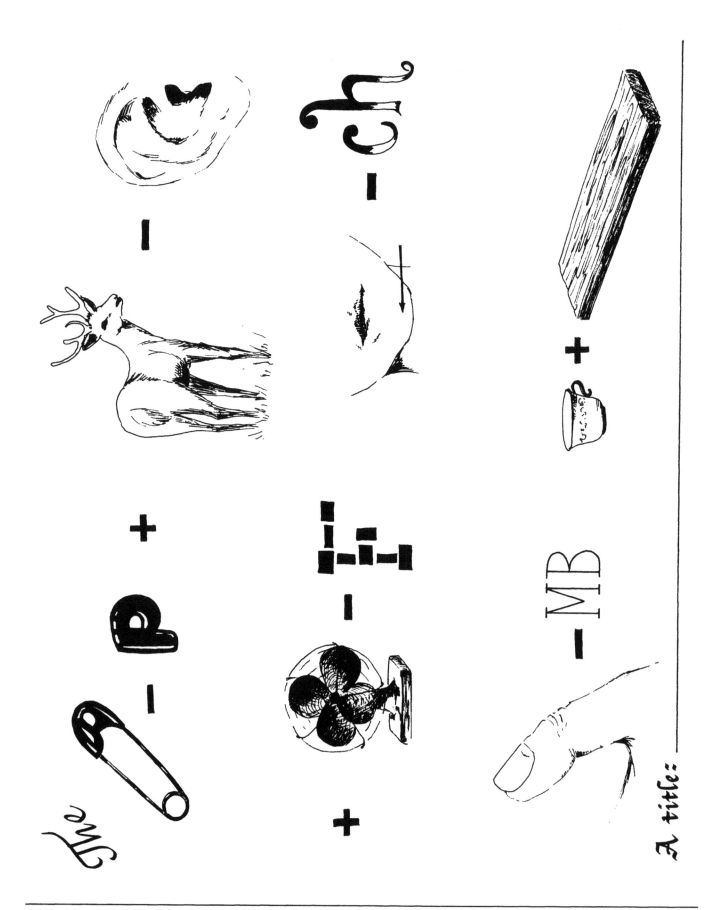

Rebuses for Readers. 1992. Teacher Ideas Press, a division of Libraries Unlimited • P.O. Box 6633 • Englewood, CO 80155-6633

30

A title: _____

Rebuses for Readers. 1992. Teacher Ideas Press, a division of Libraries Unlimited • P.O. Box 6633 • Englewood, CO 80155-6633

31

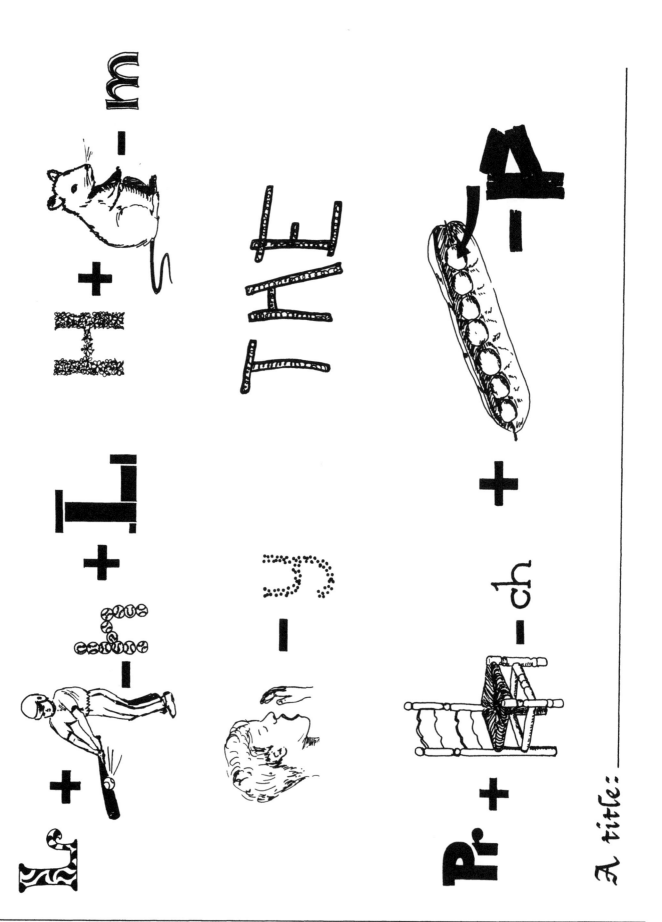

Rebuses for Readers. 1992. Teacher Ideas Press, a division of Libraries Unlimited • P.O. Box 6633 • Englewood, CO 80155-6633

32

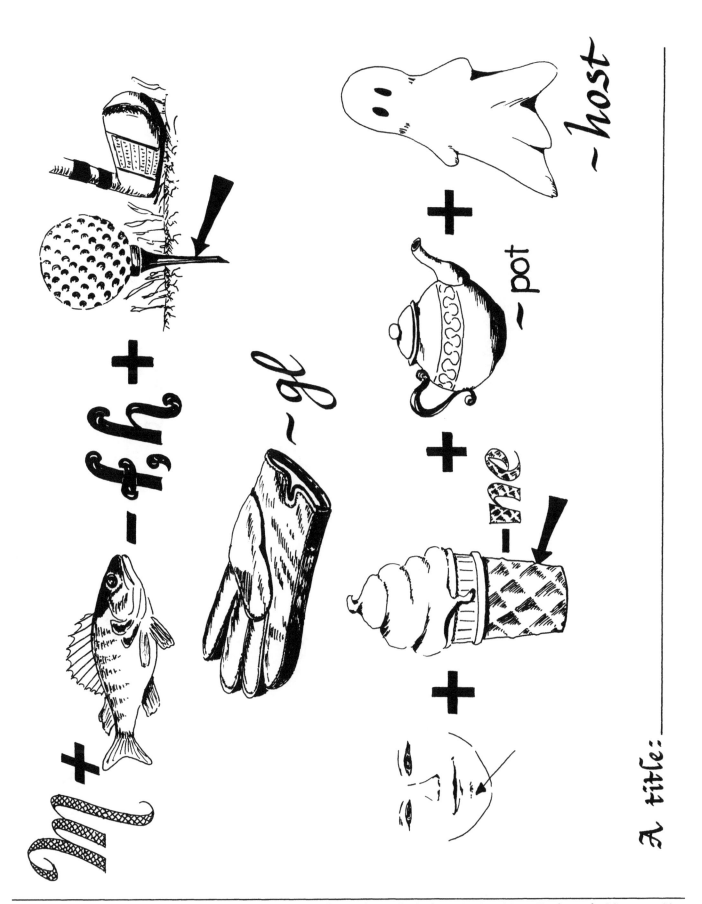

Rebuses for Readers. 1992. Teacher Ideas Press, a division of Libraries Unlimited • P.O. Box 6633 • Englewood, CO 80155-6633

33

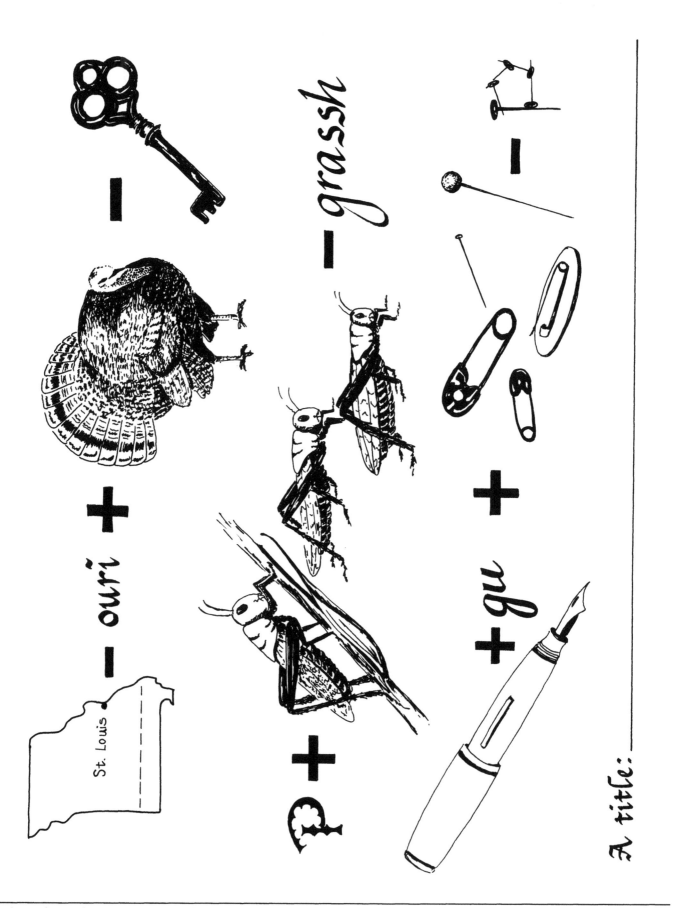

Rebuses for Readers. 1992. Teacher Ideas Press, a division of Libraries Unlimited • P.O. Box 6633 • Englewood, CO 80155-6633

34

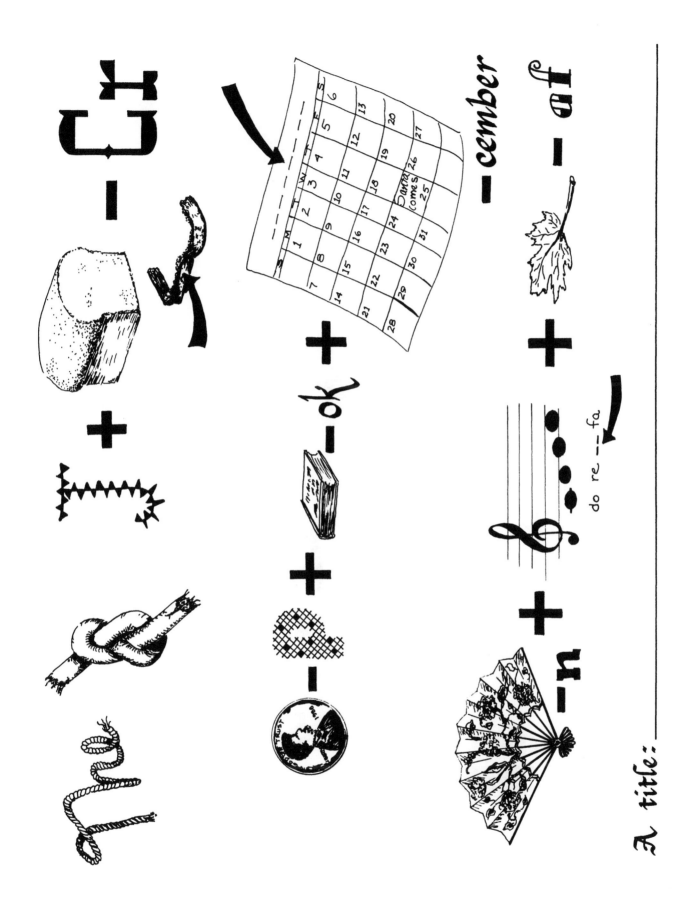

Rebuses for Readers. 1992. Teacher Ideas Press, a division of Libraries Unlimited • P.O. Box 6633 • Englewood, CO 80155-6633

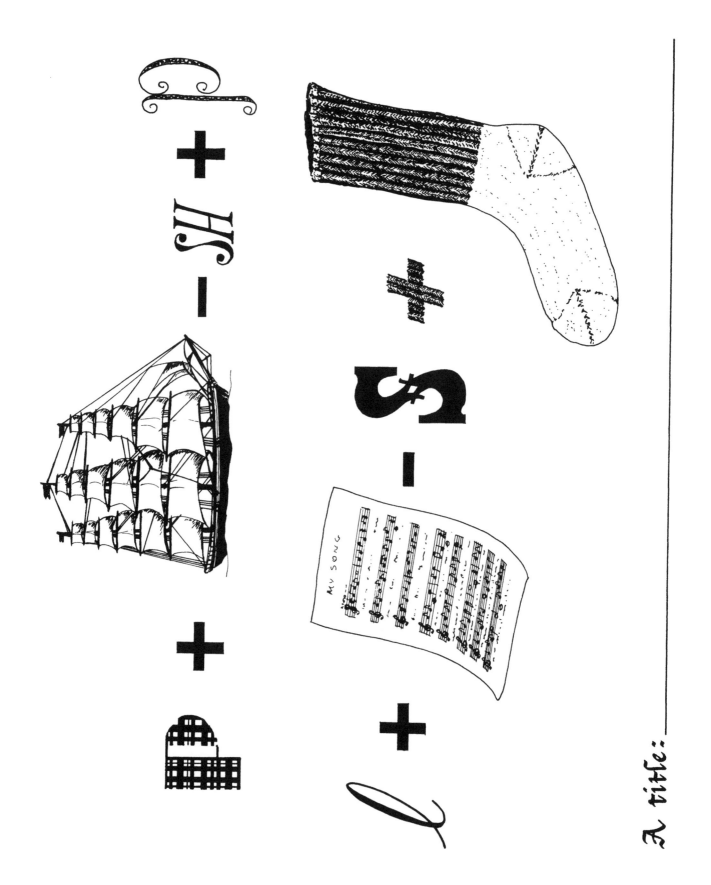

A title: _____

Rebuses for Readers. 1992. Teacher Ideas Press, a division of Libraries Unlimited • P.O. Box 6633 • Englewood, CO 80155-6633

36

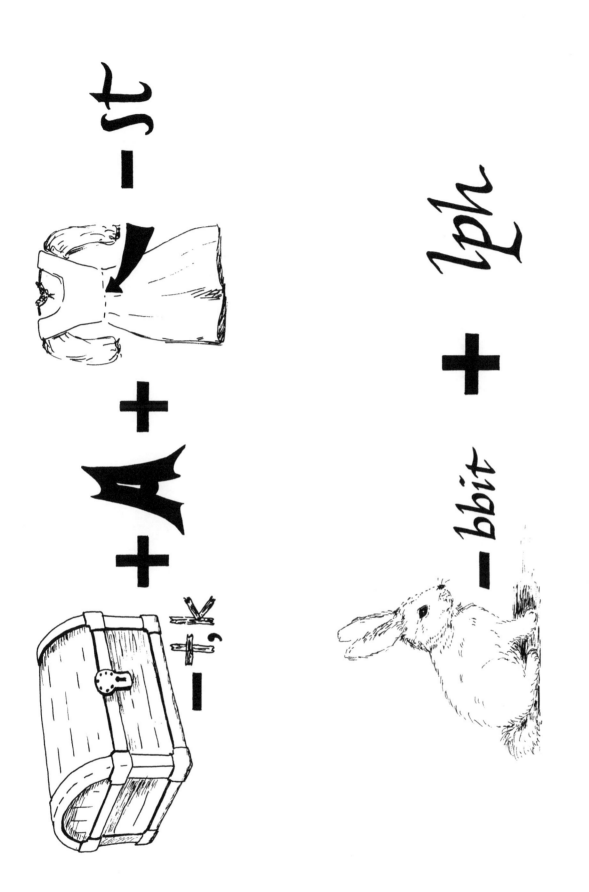

-st + 🦇 + ≠ - = lph + 🐰 -bbit

A title: _____

Rebuses for Readers. 1992. Teacher Ideas Press, a division of Libraries Unlimited • P.O. Box 6633 • Englewood, CO 80155-6633

37

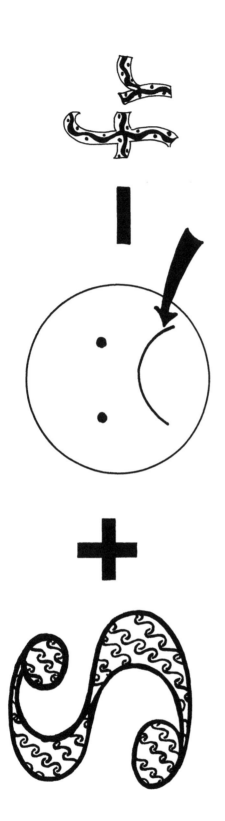

A title: _____

Rebuses for Readers. 1992. Teacher Ideas Press, a division of Libraries Unlimited • P.O. Box 6633 • Englewood, CO 80155-6633

38

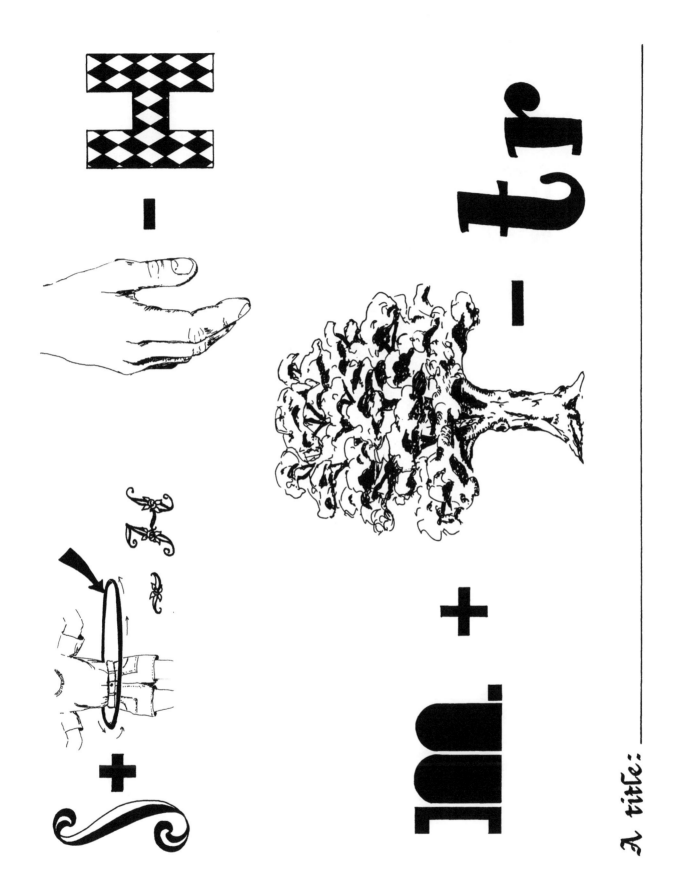

Rebuses for Readers. 1992. Teacher Ideas Press, a division of Libraries Unlimited • P.O. Box 6633 • Englewood, CO 80155-6633

39

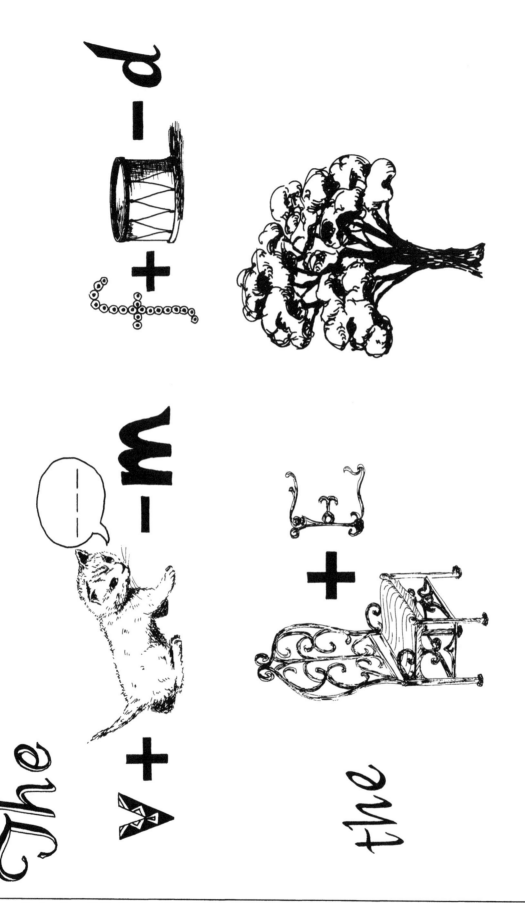

Rebuses for Readers. 1992. Teacher Ideas Press, a division of Libraries Unlimited • P.O. Box 6633 • Englewood, CO 80155-6633

40

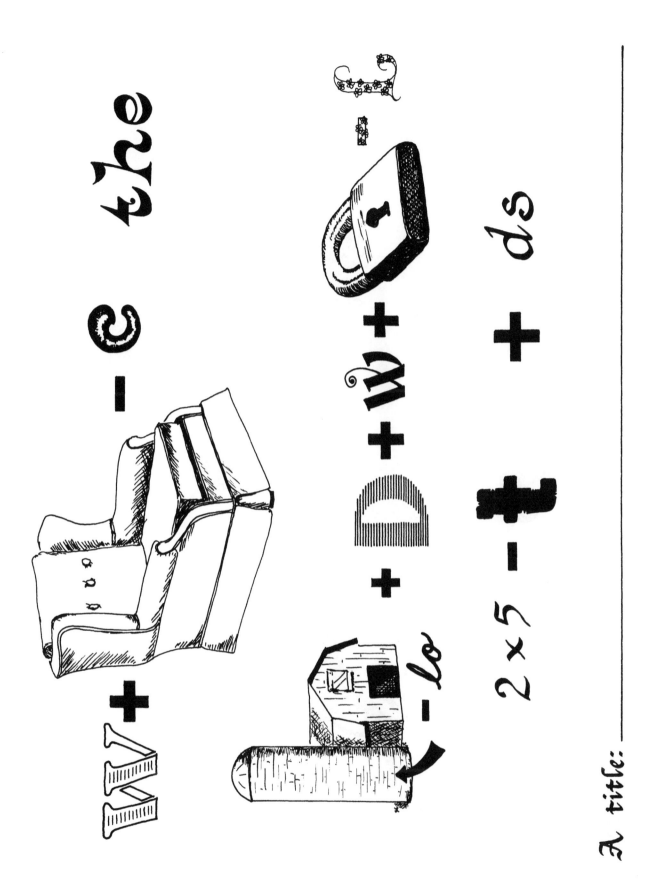

A title: _____

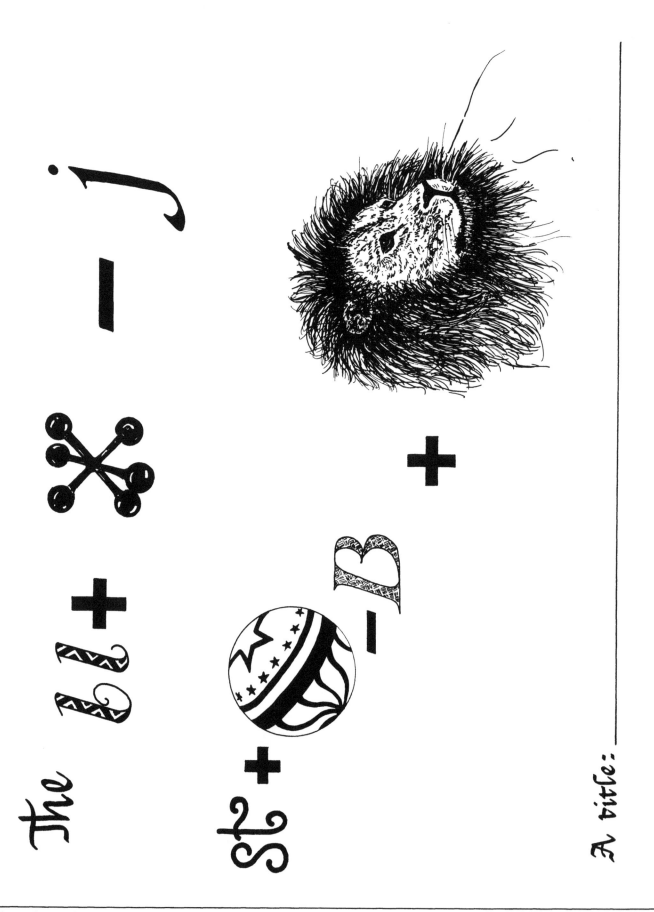

The ll + i - j

st +

A title: _____

Rebuses for Readers. 1992. Teacher Ideas Press, a division of Libraries Unlimited • P.O. Box 6633 • Englewood, CO 80155-6633

42

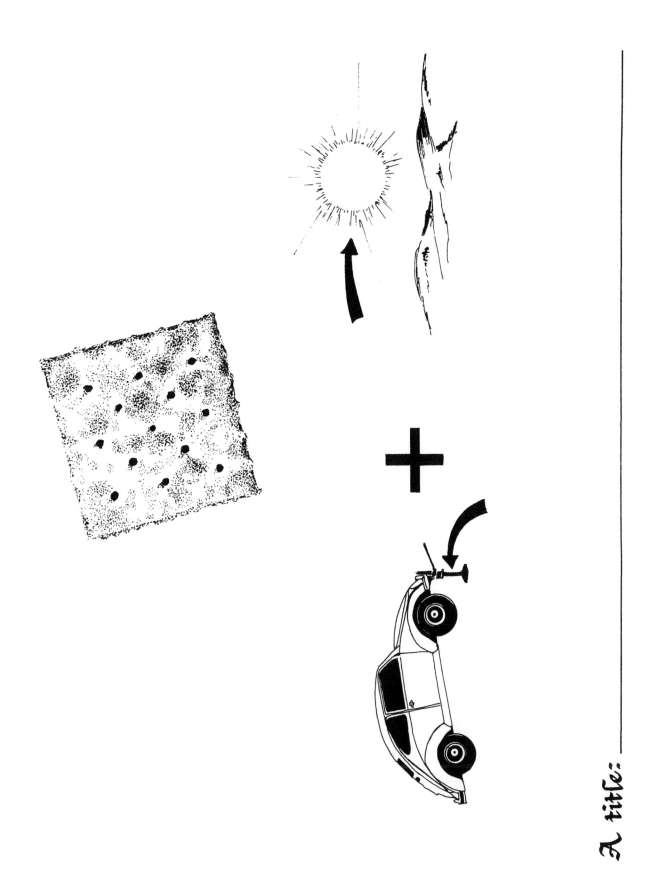

A title: _____

Rebuses for Readers. 1992. Teacher Ideas Press, a division of Libraries Unlimited • P.O. Box 6633 • Englewood, CO 80155-6633

43

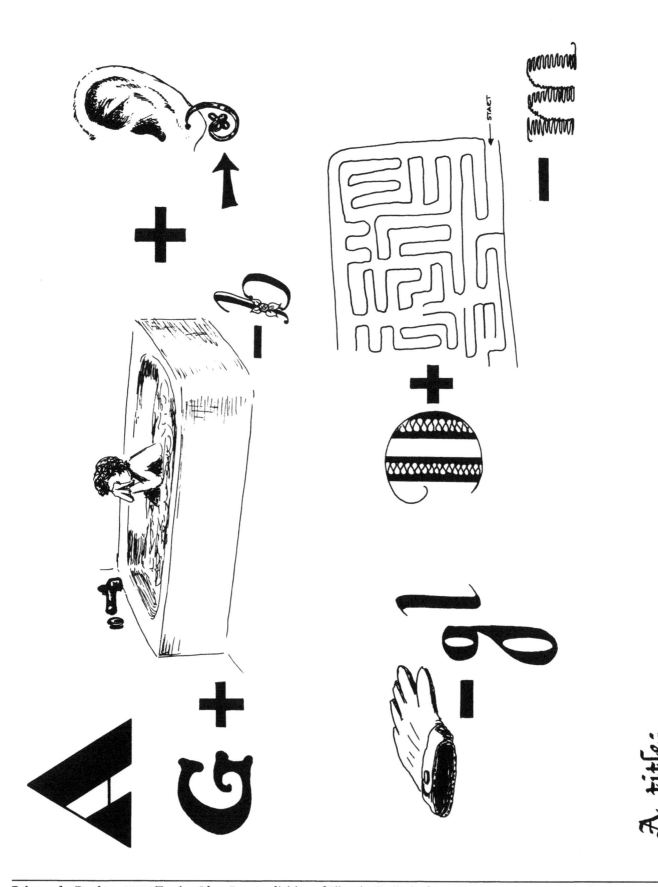

A title: _____

Rebuses for Readers. 1992. Teacher Ideas Press, a division of Libraries Unlimited • P.O. Box 6633 • Englewood, CO 80155-6633

44

A title: _____

Rebuses for Readers. 1992. Teacher Ideas Press, a division of Libraries Unlimited • P.O. Box 6633 • Englewood, CO 80155-6633

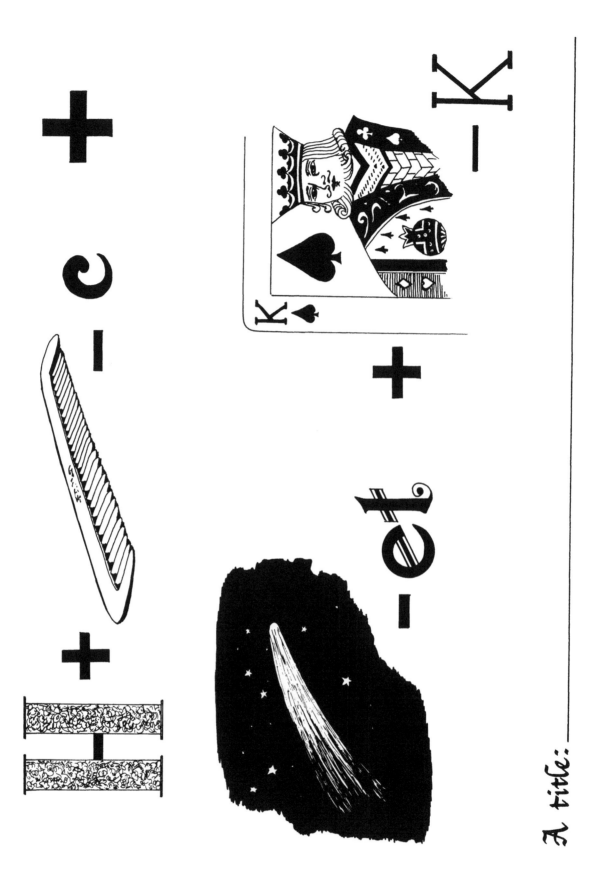

A title: _____

Rebuses for Readers. 1992. Teacher Ideas Press, a division of Libraries Unlimited • P.O. Box 6633 • Englewood, CO 80155-6633

46

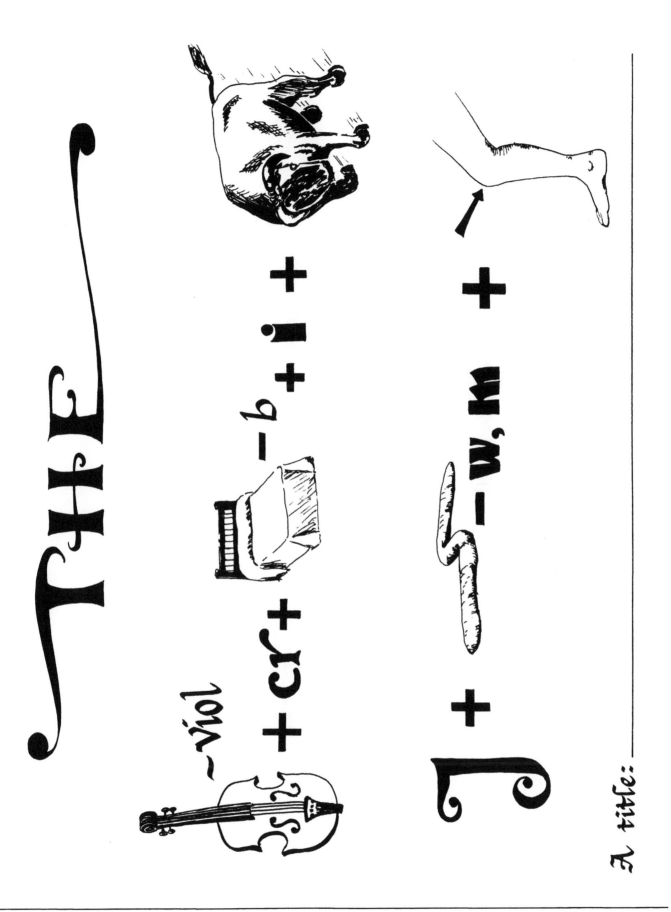

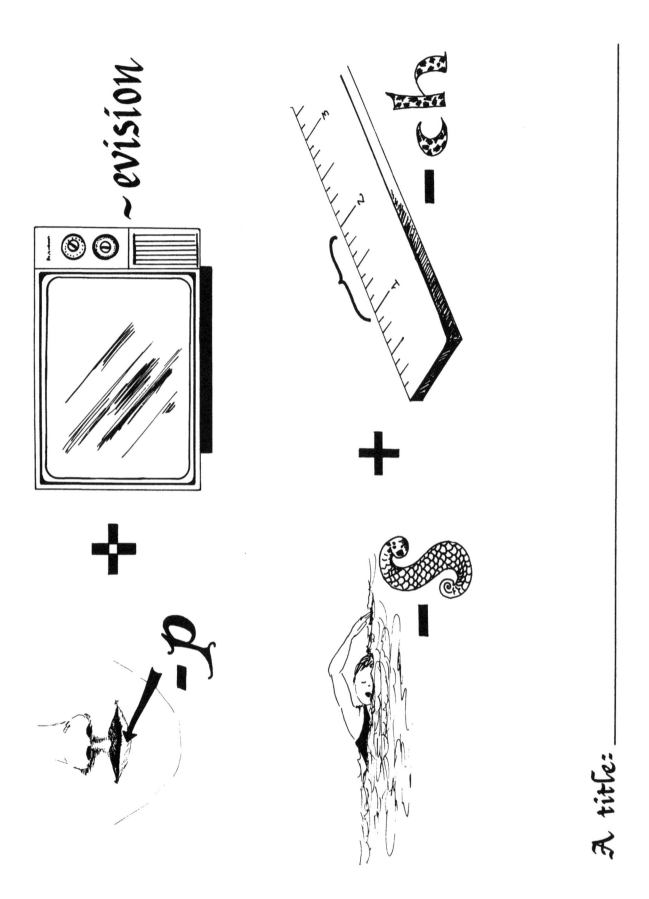

~evision

+

+

+

−

−

A title: _____

Rebuses for Readers. 1992. Teacher Ideas Press, a division of Libraries Unlimited • P.O. Box 6633 • Englewood, CO 80155-6633

48

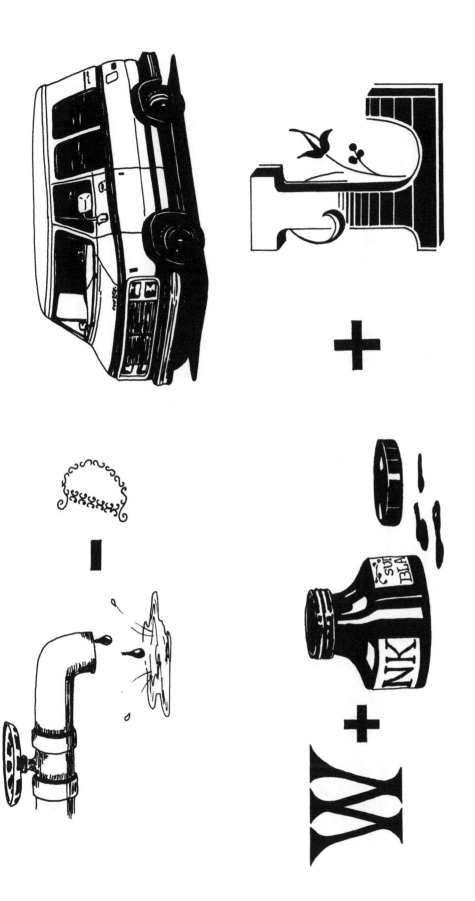

A title: _____

Rebuses for Readers. 1992. Teacher Ideas Press, a division of Libraries Unlimited • P.O. Box 6633 • Englewood, CO 80155-6633

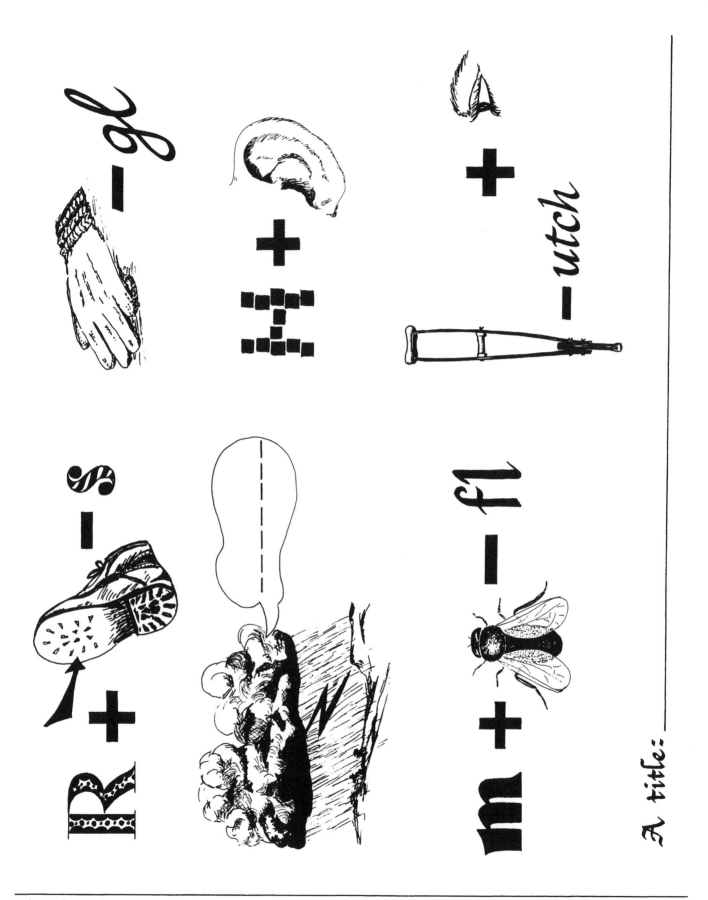

Rebuses for Readers. 1992. Teacher Ideas Press, a division of Libraries Unlimited • P.O. Box 6633 • Englewood, CO 80155-6633

50

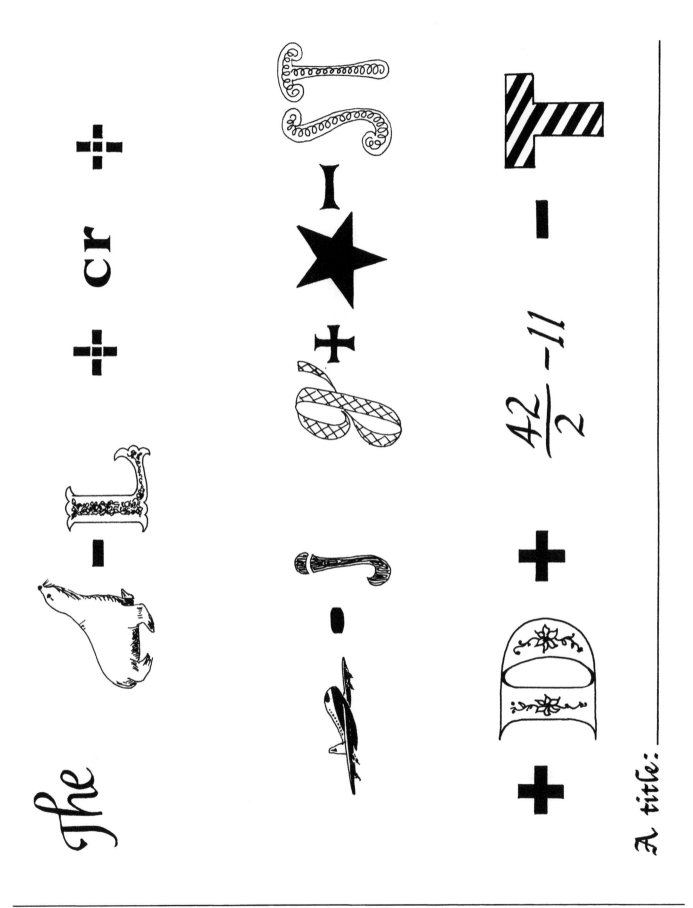

Rebuses for Readers. 1992. Teacher Ideas Press, a division of Libraries Unlimited • P.O. Box 6633 • Englewood, CO 80155-6633

51

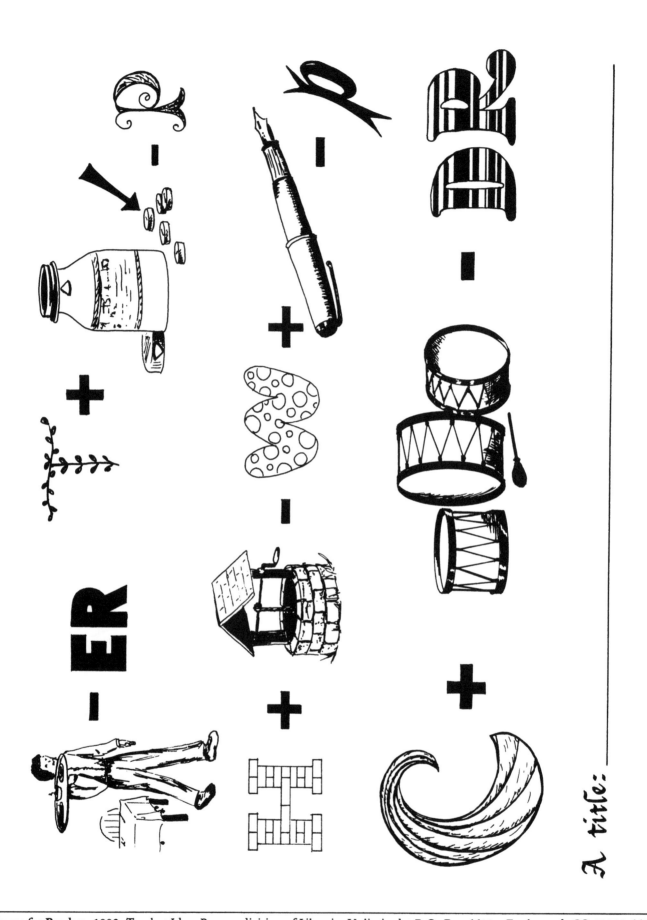

Rebuses for Readers. 1992. Teacher Ideas Press, a division of Libraries Unlimited • P.O. Box 6633 • Englewood, CO 80155-6633

52

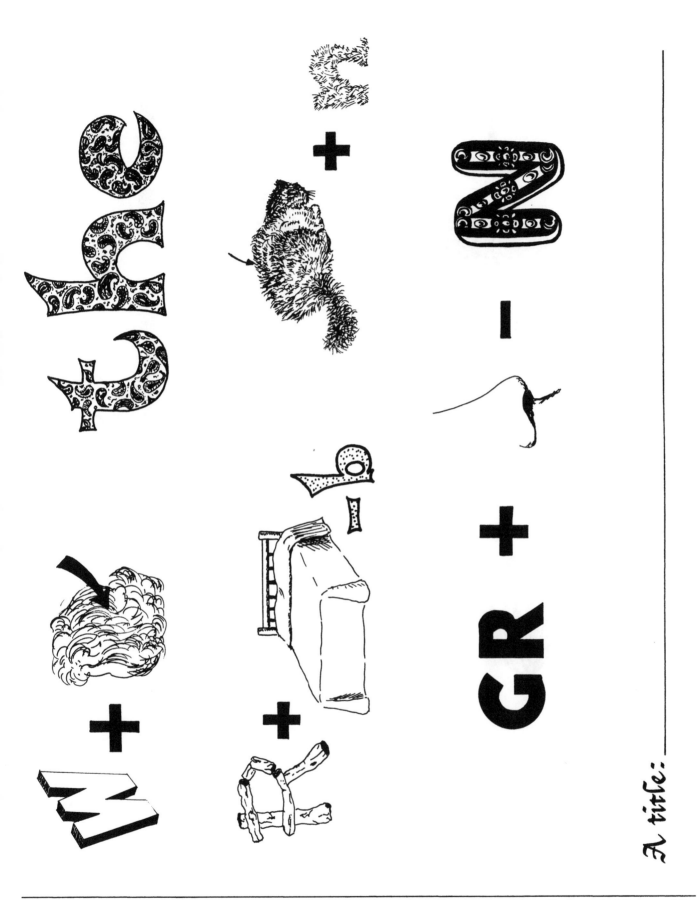

A title: _____

Rebuses for Readers. 1992. Teacher Ideas Press, a division of Libraries Unlimited • P.O. Box 6633 • Englewood, CO 80155-6633

53

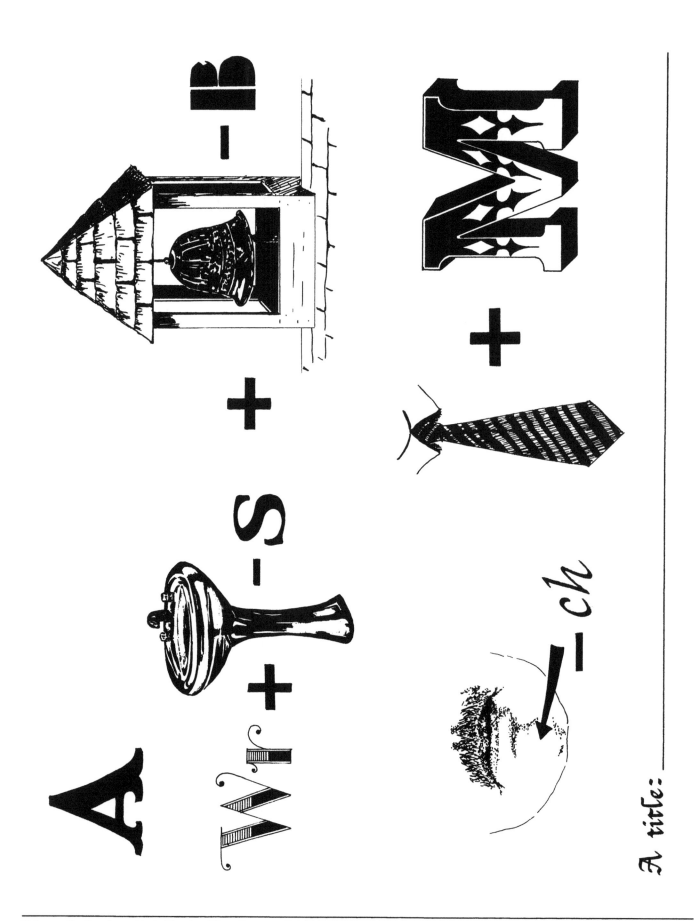

A title: _____

Rebuses for Readers. 1992. Teacher Ideas Press, a division of Libraries Unlimited • P.O. Box 6633 • Englewood, CO 80155-6633

54

2

Sixteen Authors in Rebus Form

Answers to Rebuses

For the Primary Grades

Hans C. Andersen, p. 56
Jan and Stan Berenstain, p. 57
Patricia Reilly Giff, p. 58
Bill Peet, p. 59
Daniel Pinkwater, p. 60
Shel Silverstein, p. 61
Chris Van Allsburg, p. 62

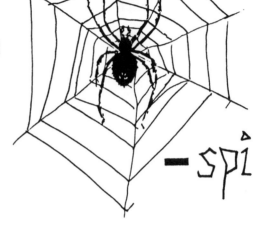

For the Intermediate Grades

Judy Blume, p. 63
Beverly Cleary, p. 64

Lois Lowry, p. 65
E. B. White, p. 66
Laura Ingalls Wilder, p. 67

For the Upper Grades

Lynn Reid Banks, p. 68
Betsy Byars, p. 69

Katherine Paterson, p. 70
Mark Twain, p. 71

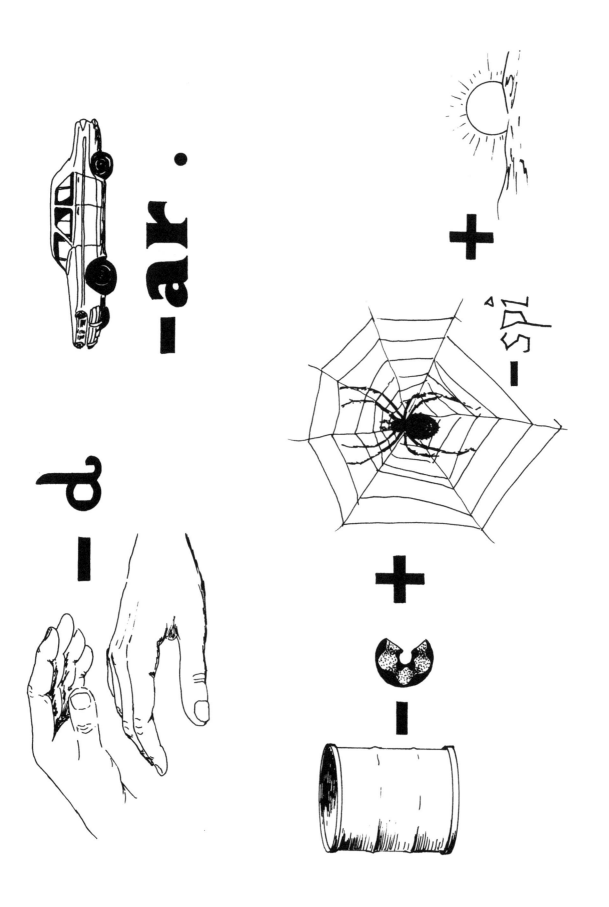

Rebuses for Readers. 1992. Teacher Ideas Press, a division of Libraries Unlimited • P.O. Box 6633 • Englewood, CO 80155-6633

56

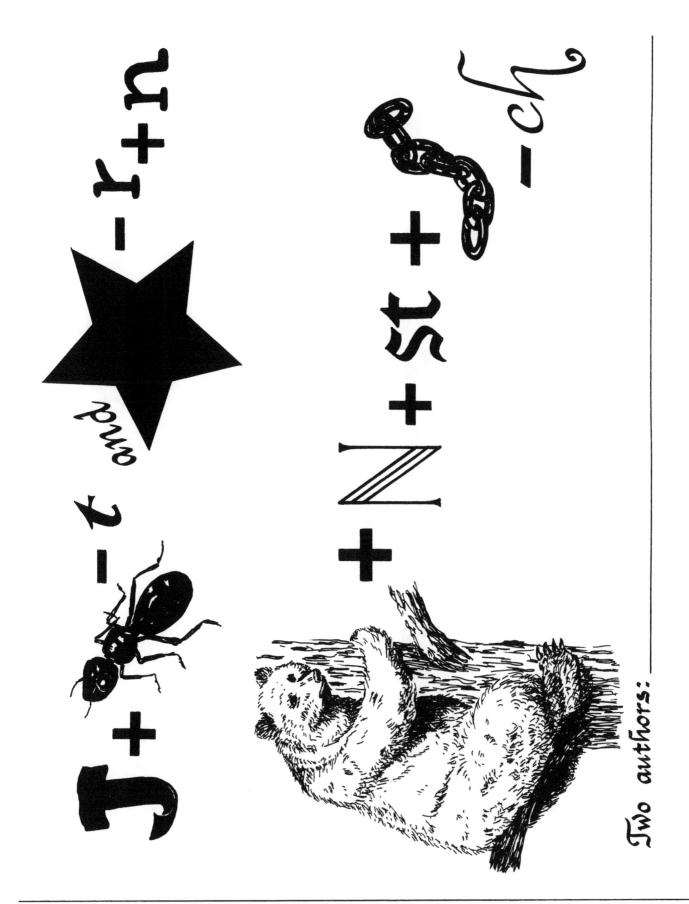

Rebuses for Readers. 1992. Teacher Ideas Press, a division of Libraries Unlimited • P.O. Box 6633 • Englewood, CO 80155-6633

57

Rebuses for Readers. 1992. Teacher Ideas Press, a division of Libraries Unlimited • P.O. Box 6633 • Englewood, CO 80155-6633

58

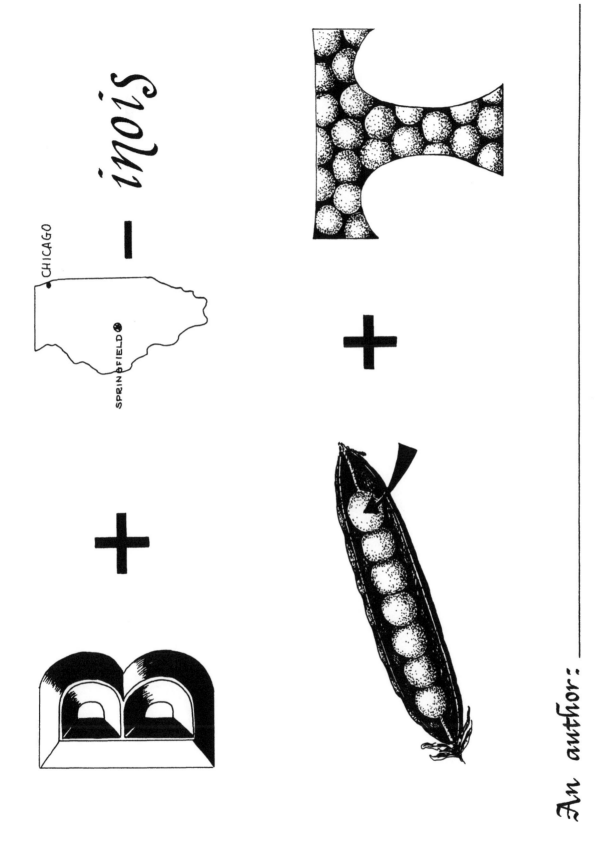

An author: _____

Rebuses for Readers. 1992. Teacher Ideas Press, a division of Libraries Unlimited • P.O. Box 6633 • Englewood, CO 80155-6633

59

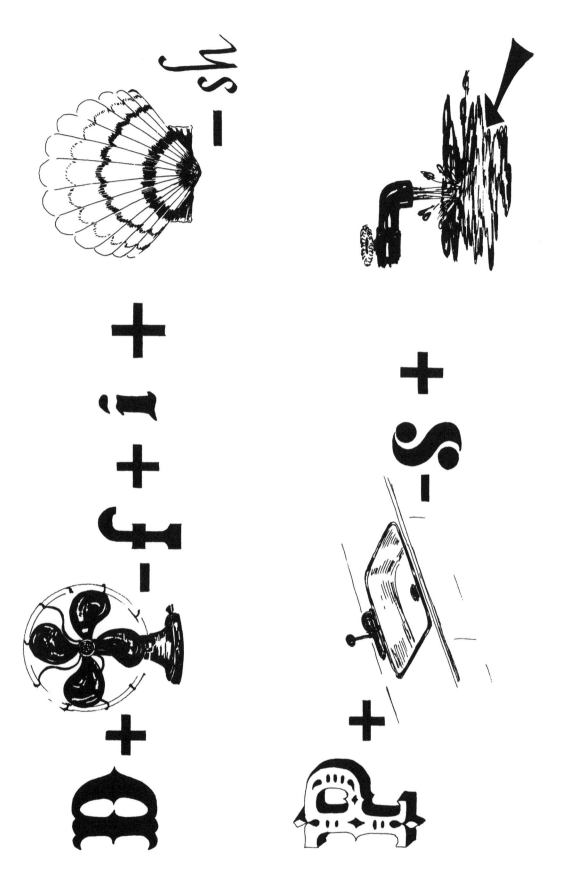

An author: _____

Rebuses for Readers. 1992. Teacher Ideas Press, a division of Libraries Unlimited • P.O. Box 6633 • Englewood, CO 80155-6633

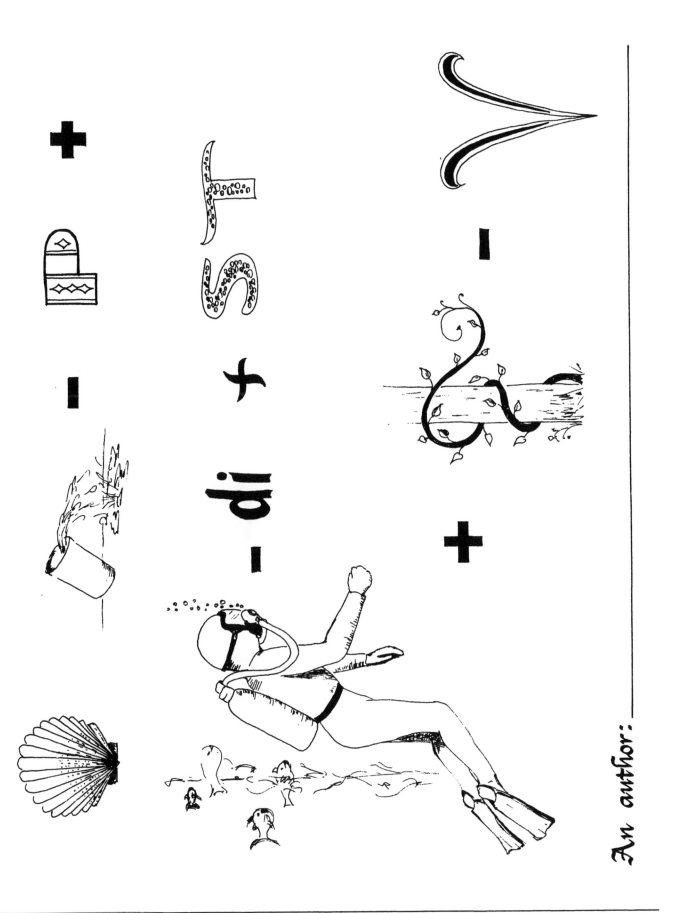

Rebuses for Readers. 1992. Teacher Ideas Press, a division of Libraries Unlimited • P.O. Box 6633 • Englewood, CO 80155-6633

61

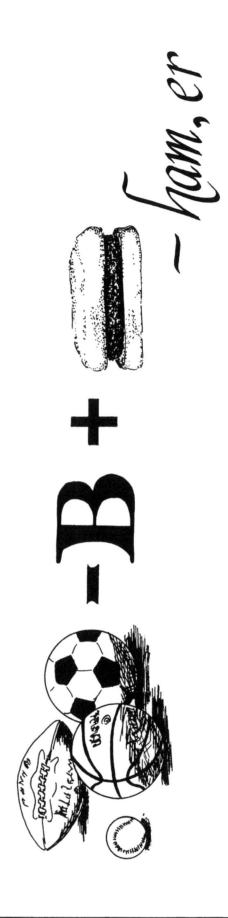

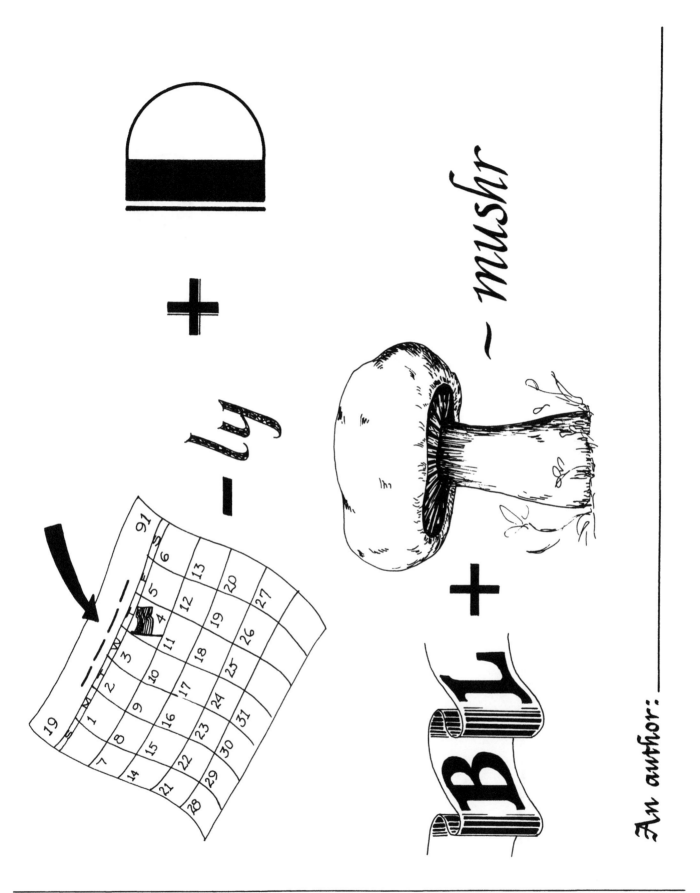

+ - ly ~ mushr + An author:

Rebuses for Readers. 1992. Teacher Ideas Press, a division of Libraries Unlimited • P.O. Box 6633 • Englewood, CO 80155-6633

63

Rebuses for Readers. 1992. Teacher Ideas Press, a division of Libraries Unlimited • P.O. Box 6633 • Englewood, CO 80155-6633

An author: _____

Rebuses for Readers. 1992. Teacher Ideas Press, a division of Libraries Unlimited • P.O. Box 6633 • Englewood, CO 80155-6633

65

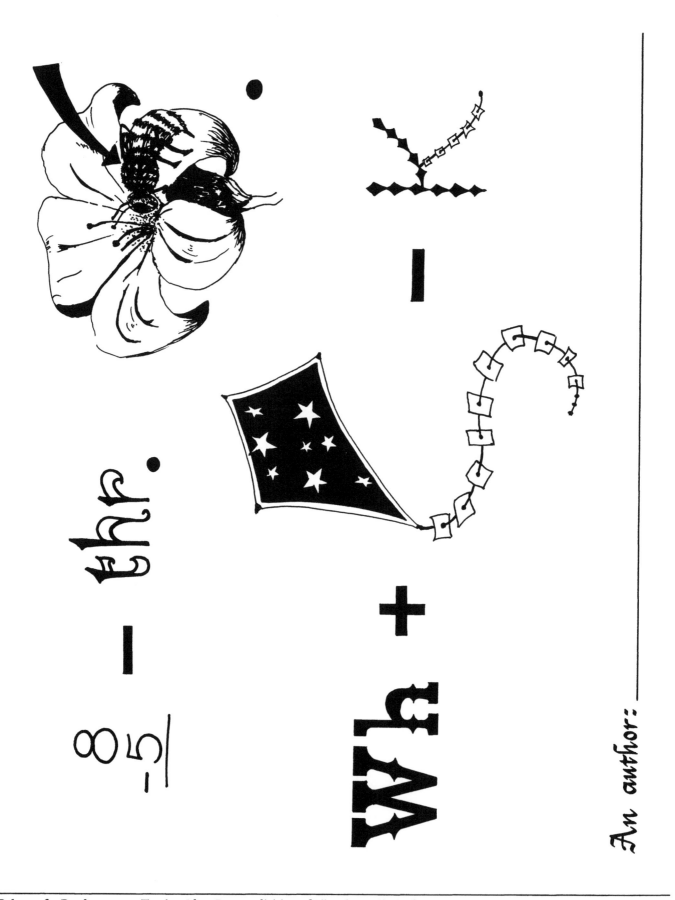

An author: _____

Rebuses for Readers. 1992. Teacher Ideas Press, a division of Libraries Unlimited • P.O. Box 6633 • Englewood, CO 80155-6633

66

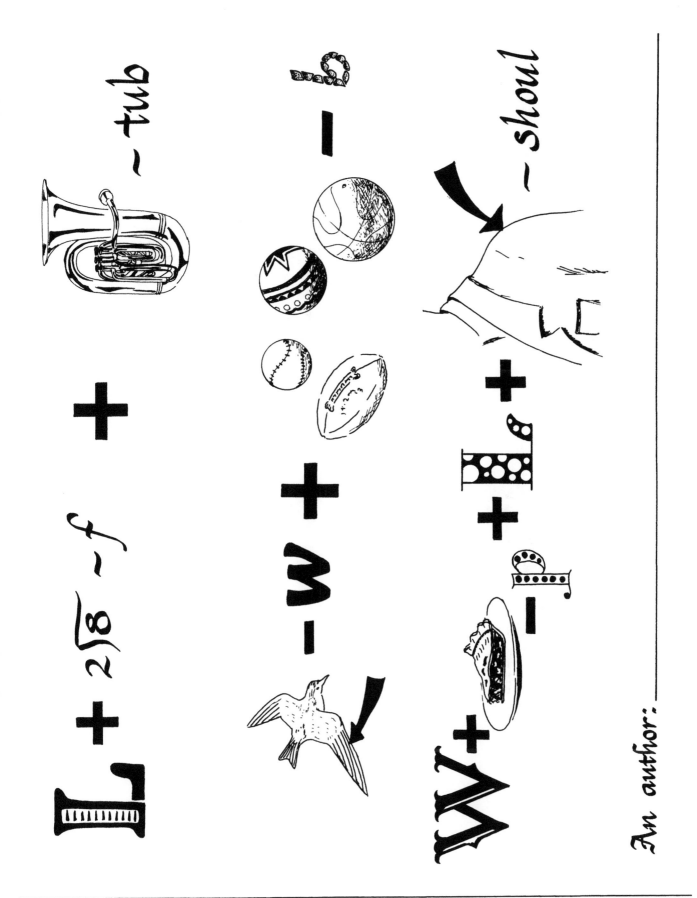

An author: _____

Rebuses for Readers. 1992. Teacher Ideas Press, a division of Libraries Unlimited • P.O. Box 6633 • Englewood, CO 80155-6633

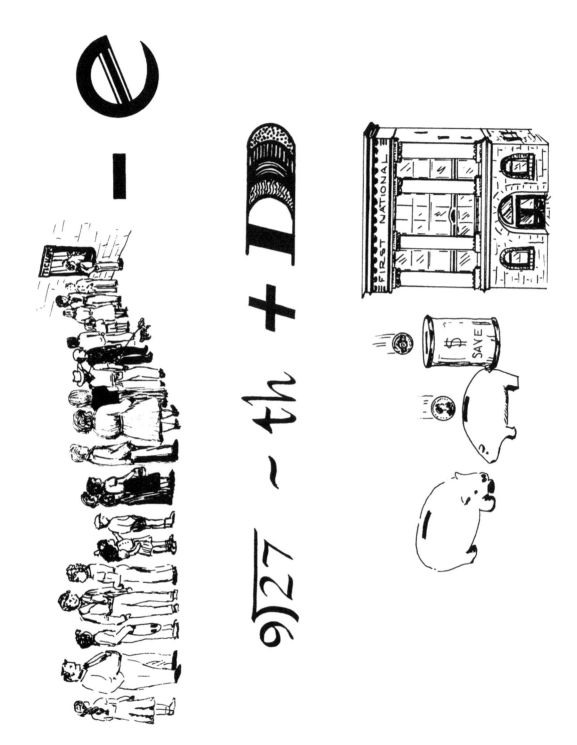

FIRST NATIONAL

SAVE

$

An author: _____

Rebuses for Readers. 1992. Teacher Ideas Press, a division of Libraries Unlimited • P.O. Box 6633 • Englewood, CO 80155-6633

68

+

ABCDEFGHIJKLMNOPQRSTUVWXYZ – alpha

+

-cycle

An author: _____

Rebuses for Readers. 1992. Teacher Ideas Press, a division of Libraries Unlimited • P.O. Box 6633 • Englewood, CO 80155-6633

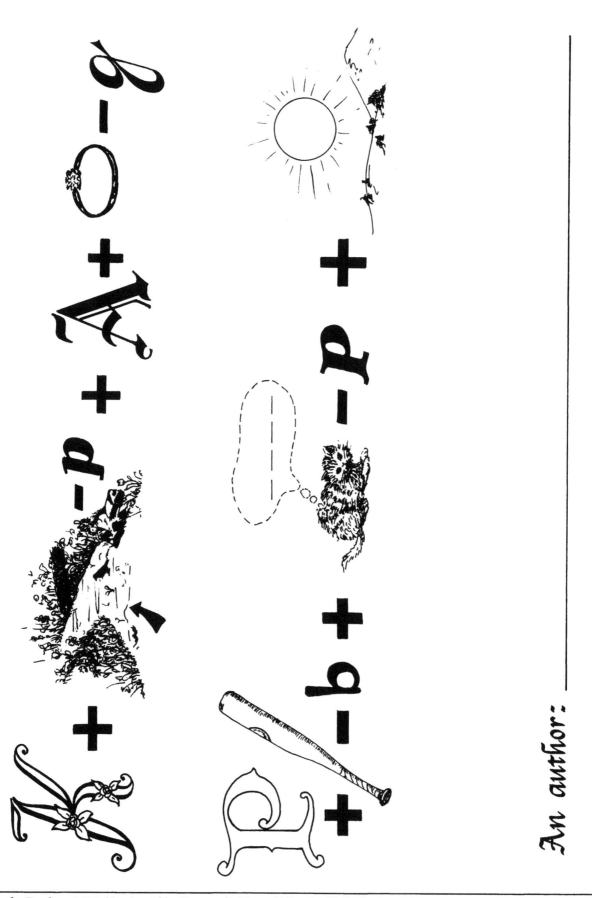

An author: _____

Rebuses for Readers. 1992. Teacher Ideas Press, a division of Libraries Unlimited • P.O. Box 6633 • Englewood, CO 80155-6633

70

An author:

Rebuses for Readers. 1992. Teacher Ideas Press, a division of Libraries Unlimited • P.O. Box 6633 • Englewood, CO 80155-6633

71

3

Fifteen Characters in Rebus Form

Answers to Rebuses

For the Primary Grades

Amelia Bedelia (*Amelia Bedelia*, Peggy Parish), p. 73
Mr. and Mrs. Mallard (*Make Way for Ducklings*, Robert McCloskey),
    p. 74
Rumpelstiltskin, (*Rumpelstiltskin*, Jacob and Wilhelm Grimm),
    p. 75

For the Intermediate Grades

Jane and Michael Banks (*Mary Poppins*, P. L. Travers),
    p. 76
Encyclopedia Brown (*Encyclopedia Brown*, Donald
    Sobol), p. 77
Charlie Bucket (*Charlie and the Chocolate Factory*,
    Roald Dahl), p. 78
Fudge Hatcher (*Tales of a Fourth Grade Nothing*,
    Judy Blume), p. 79

Gladys Herdman (*The Best Christmas Pageant Ever*,
    Barbara Robinson), p. 80
Pa and Ma Ingalls (*Little House on the Prairie*, Laura
    Ingalls Wilder), p. 81
Ramona Quimby (*Ramona the Pest*, Beverly Cleary),
    p. 82
Wilbur the Pig (*Charlotte's Web*, E. B. White),
    p. 83

For the Upper Grades

Meg, Jo, Beth, and Amy (*Little Women*, Louisa May
    Alcott), p. 84
Mrs. Who, Mrs. Which, and Mrs. Whatsit, (*A Wrinkle
    in Time*, Madeleine L'Engle), p. 85

Omri and Little Bear (*The Indian in the Cupboard*,
    Lynn Reid Banks), p. 86
Dicey Tillerman (*Homecoming*, Cynthia Voigt),
    p. 87

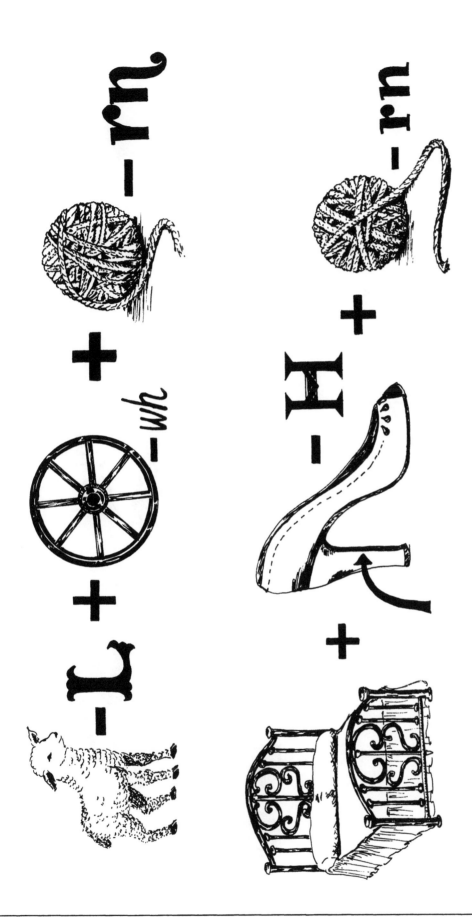

A character: _____

Rebuses for Readers. 1992. Teacher Ideas Press, a division of Libraries Unlimited • P.O. Box 6633 • Englewood, CO 80155-6633

73

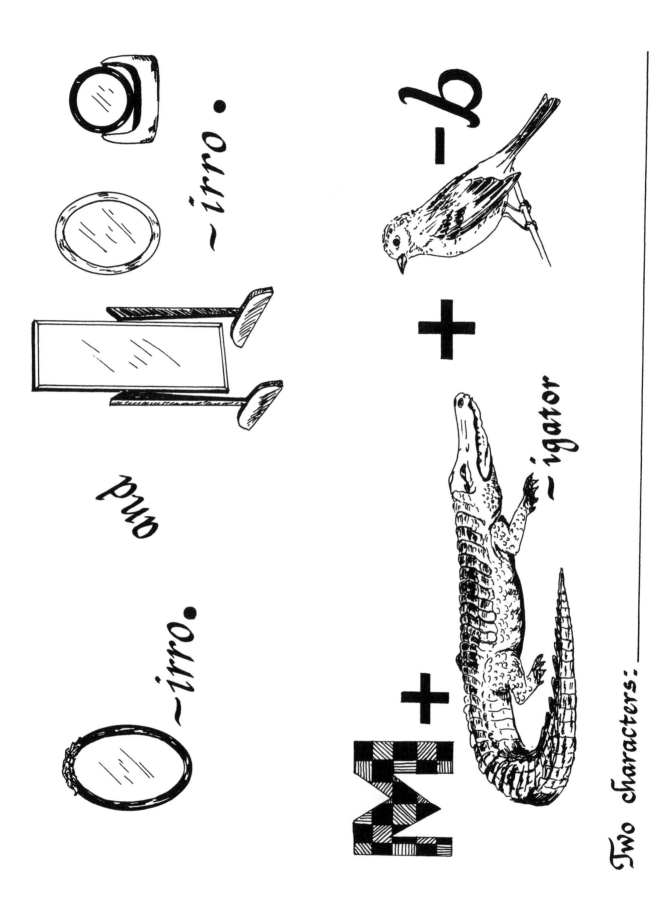

~irro.

~irro.

b-

+

~igator

M+

and

Two characters: _____

Rebuses for Readers. 1992. Teacher Ideas Press, a division of Libraries Unlimited • P.O. Box 6633 • Englewood, CO 80155-6633

74

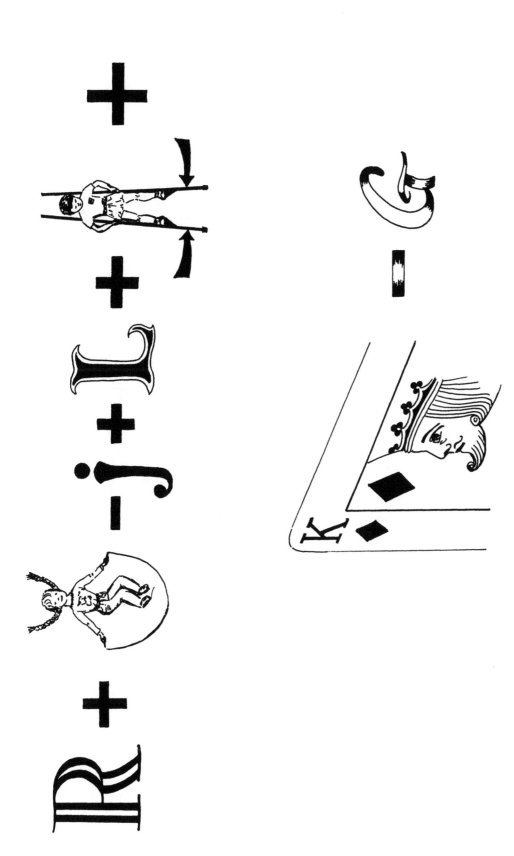

A character: _____

Rebuses for Readers. 1992. Teacher Ideas Press, a division of Libraries Unlimited • P.O. Box 6633 • Englewood, CO 80155-6633

75

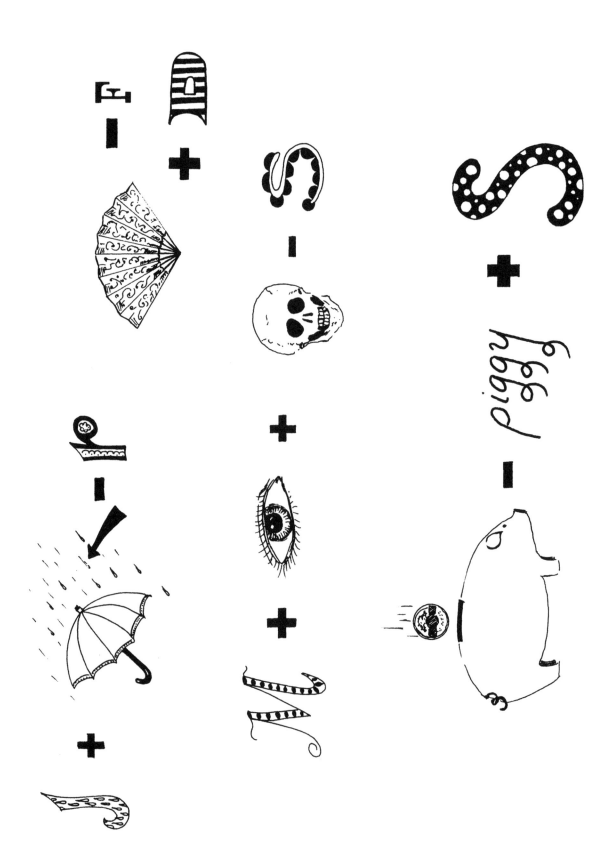

Rebuses for Readers. 1992. Teacher Ideas Press, a division of Libraries Unlimited • P.O. Box 6633 • Englewood, CO 80155-6633

A character: _____

Rebuses for Readers. 1992. Teacher Ideas Press, a division of Libraries Unlimited • P.O. Box 6633 • Englewood, CO 80155-6633

77

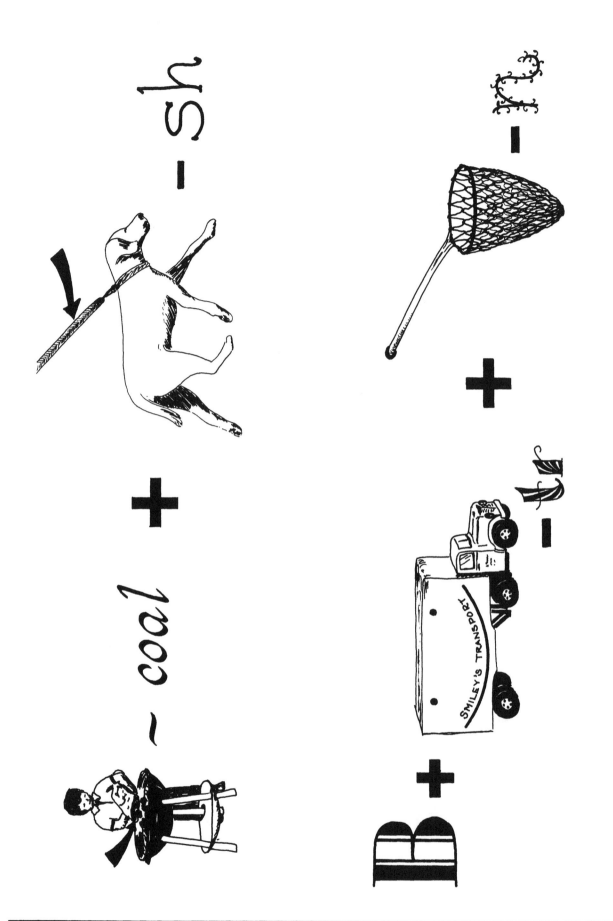

-sh + ~ coal

-ti + -tr + B +

A character:

Rebuses for Readers. 1992. Teacher Ideas Press, a division of Libraries Unlimited • P.O. Box 6633 • Englewood, CO 80155-6633

78

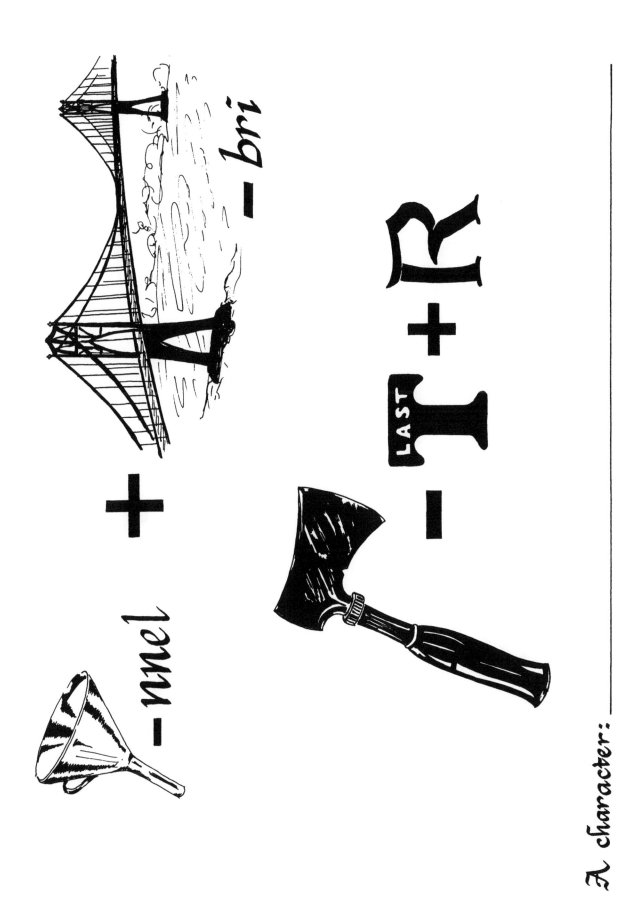

A character: _____

Rebuses for Readers. 1992. Teacher Ideas Press, a division of Libraries Unlimited • P.O. Box 6633 • Englewood, CO 80155-6633

79

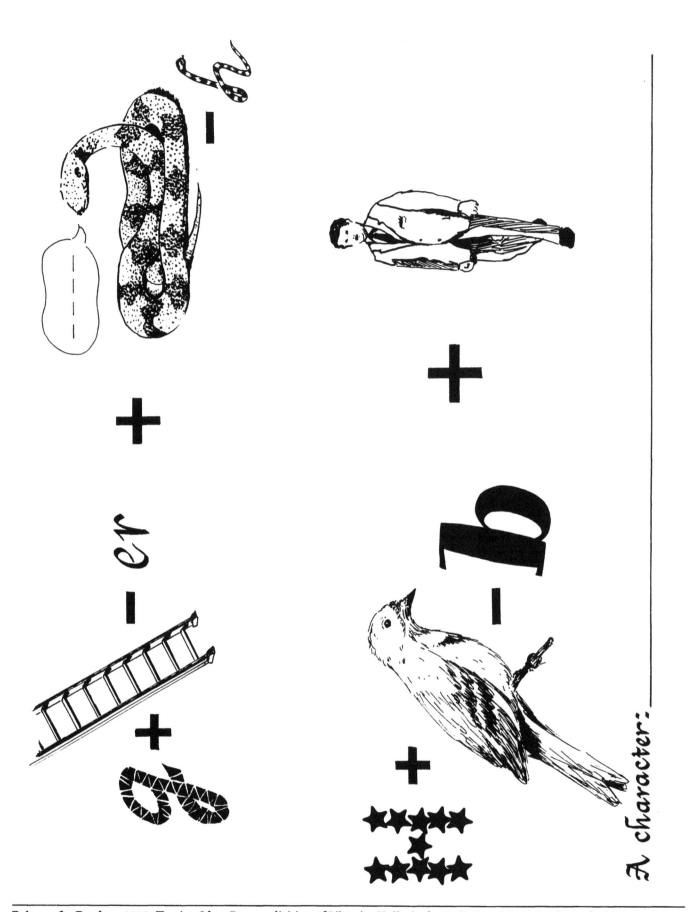

Rebuses for Readers. 1992. Teacher Ideas Press, a division of Libraries Unlimited • P.O. Box 6633 • Englewood, CO 80155-6633

80

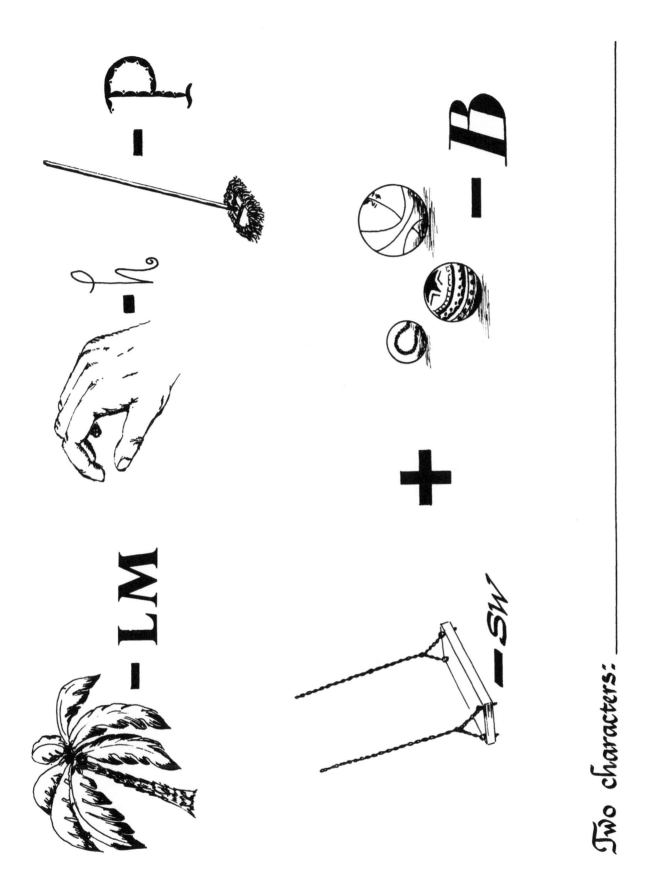

Two characters: _____

Rebuses for Readers. 1992. Teacher Ideas Press, a division of Libraries Unlimited • P.O. Box 6633 • Englewood, CO 80155-6633

81

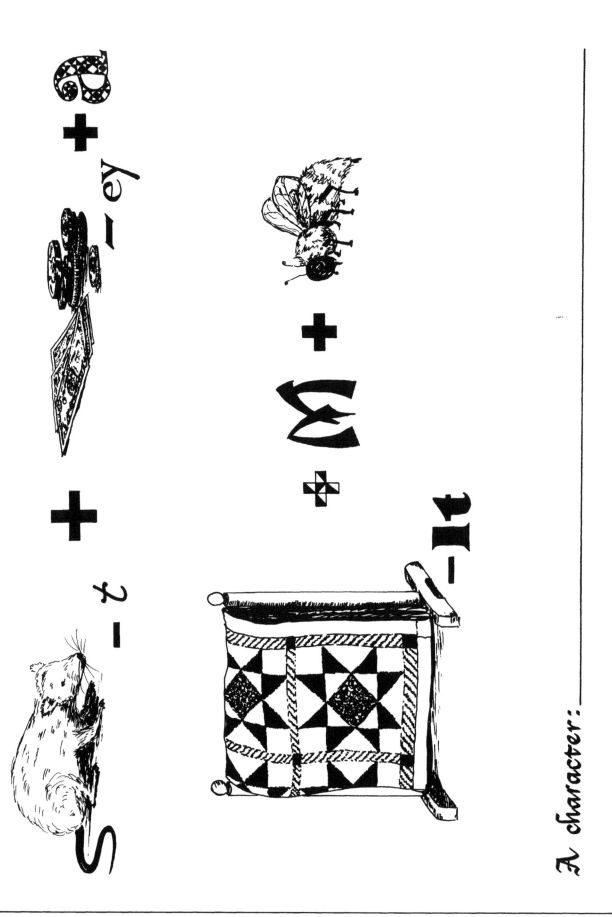

A character: _____

Rebuses for Readers. 1992. Teacher Ideas Press, a division of Libraries Unlimited • P.O. Box 6633 • Englewood, CO 80155-6633

82

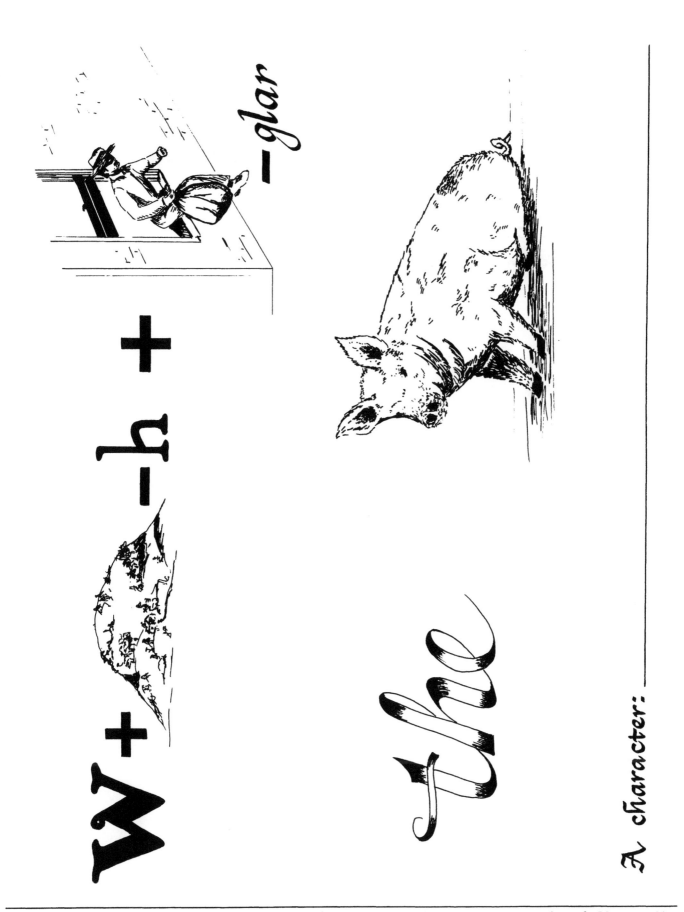

-glar

+ h -

W +

the

A character: _____

Rebuses for Readers. 1992. Teacher Ideas Press, a division of Libraries Unlimited • P.O. Box 6633 • Englewood, CO 80155-6633

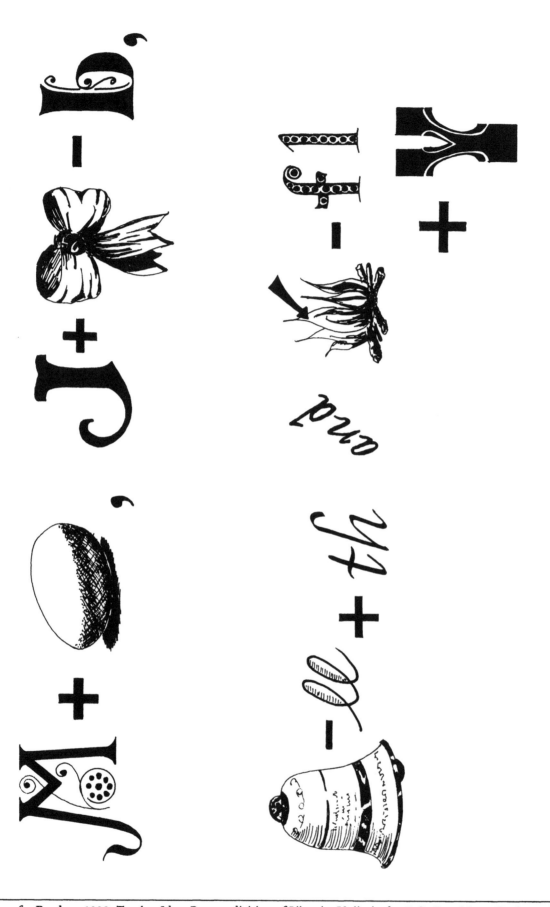

Rebuses for Readers. 1992. Teacher Ideas Press, a division of Libraries Unlimited • P.O. Box 6633 • Englewood, CO 80155-6633

84

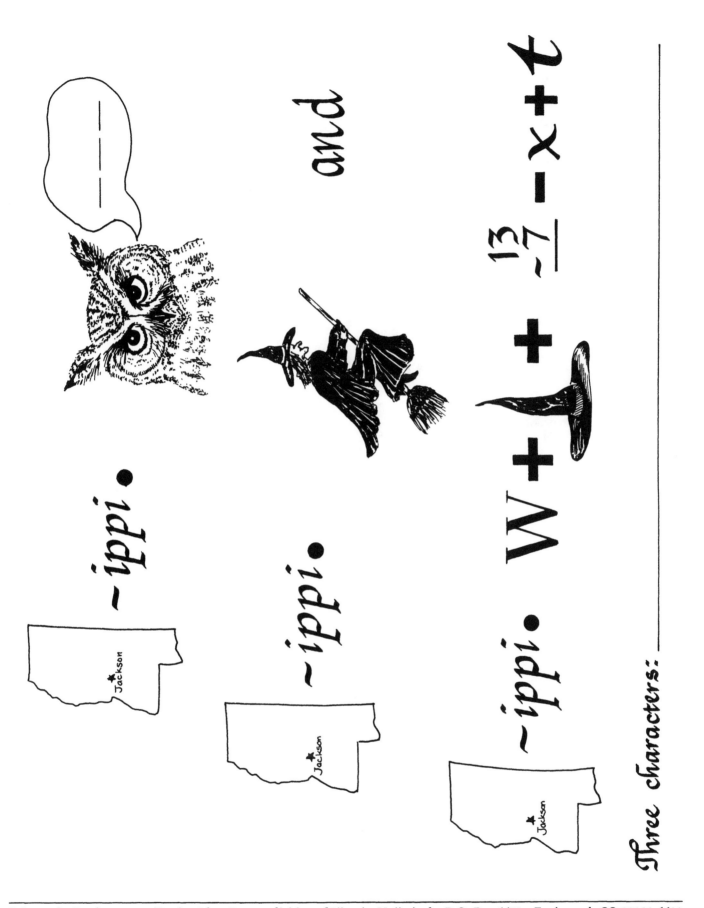

Three characters: _____

Rebuses for Readers. 1992. Teacher Ideas Press, a division of Libraries Unlimited • P.O. Box 6633 • Englewood, CO 80155-6633

85

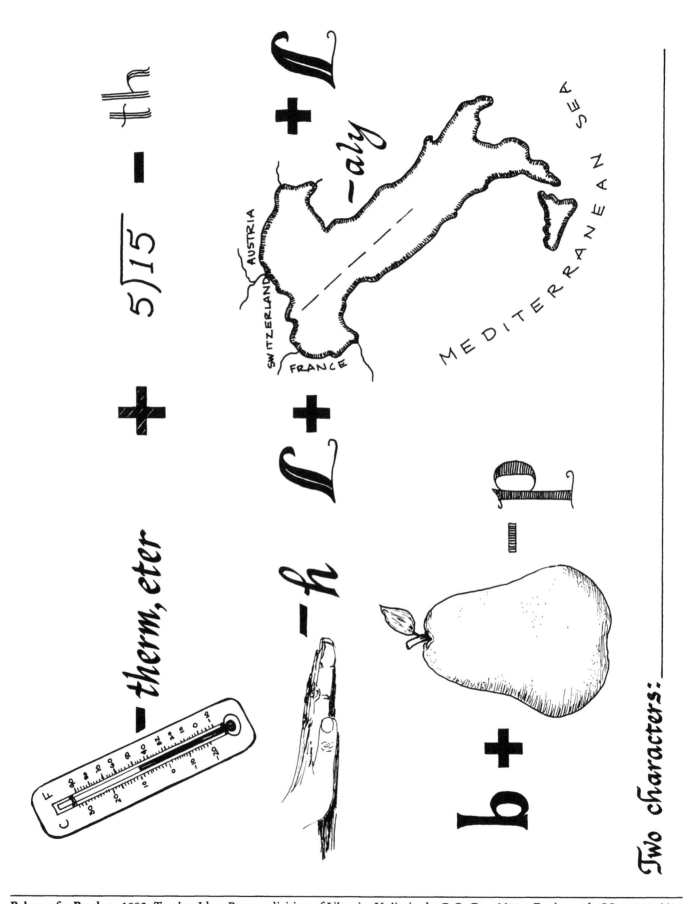

−therm, eter + 5)15 − th

L + −aly +

L −h + b + = P

MEDITERRANEAN SEA

AUSTRIA
SWITZERLAND
FRANCE

Two characters:

Rebuses for Readers. 1992. Teacher Ideas Press, a division of Libraries Unlimited • P.O. Box 6633 • Englewood, CO 80155-6633

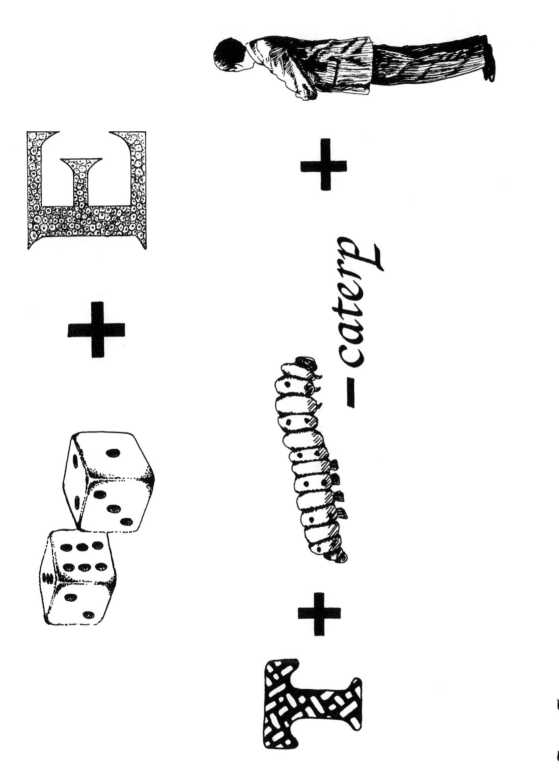

A character: _____

Rebuses for Readers. 1992. Teacher Ideas Press, a division of Libraries Unlimited • P.O. Box 6633 • Englewood, CO 80155-6633

87

4

Ten Settings in Rebus Form

Answers to Rebuses

Klickitat Street (*Henry Huggins, Ramona the Pest*, Beverly Cleary),
  p. 89
Never-Land (*Peter Pan*, Sir James Barrie), p. 90
Toad Hall (*The Wind in the Willows*, Kenneth Grahame), p. 91
Chincoteague Island (*Misty of Chincoteague*, Marguerite Henry),
  p. 92
Wonderland (*Alice's Adventures in Wonderland*, Lewis Carroll),
  p. 93
Land of Oz (*The Wizard of Oz*, L. Frank Baum), p. 94
Narnia (*The Lion, the Witch, and the Wardrobe*, C. S. Lewis),
  p. 95
Terabithia (*Bridge to Terabithia*, Katherine Paterson), p. 96
New York Metropolitan Museum of Art (*From the Mixed-Up Files
  of Mrs. Basil E. Frankweiler*, E. L. Konigsburg), p. 97
Tree in the Catskill Mountains (*My Side of the Mountain*, Jean
  George), p. 98

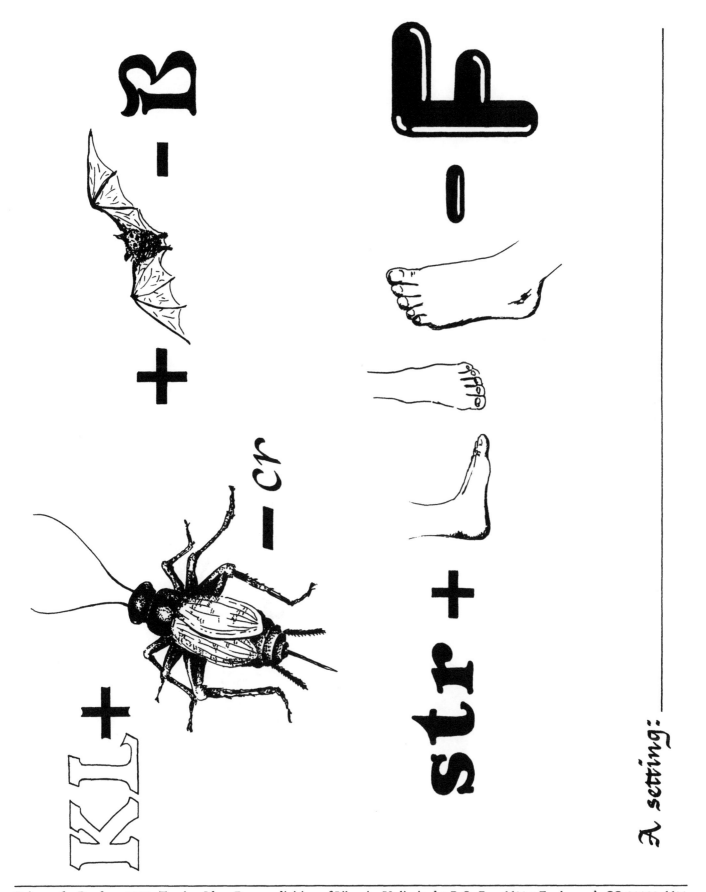

Rebuses for Readers. 1992. Teacher Ideas Press, a division of Libraries Unlimited • P.O. Box 6633 • Englewood, CO 80155-6633

89

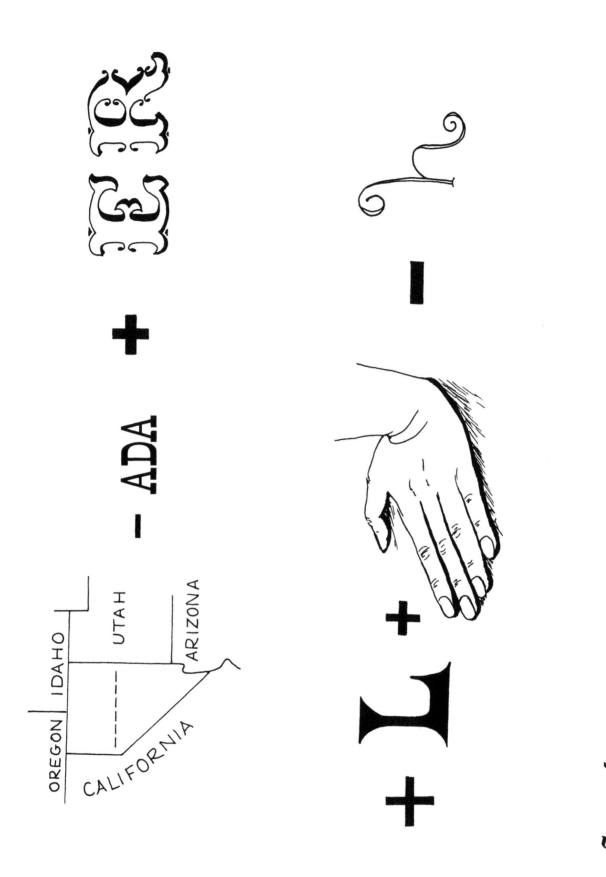

A setting: _____

Rebuses for Readers. 1992. Teacher Ideas Press, a division of Libraries Unlimited • P.O. Box 6633 • Englewood, CO 80155-6633

90

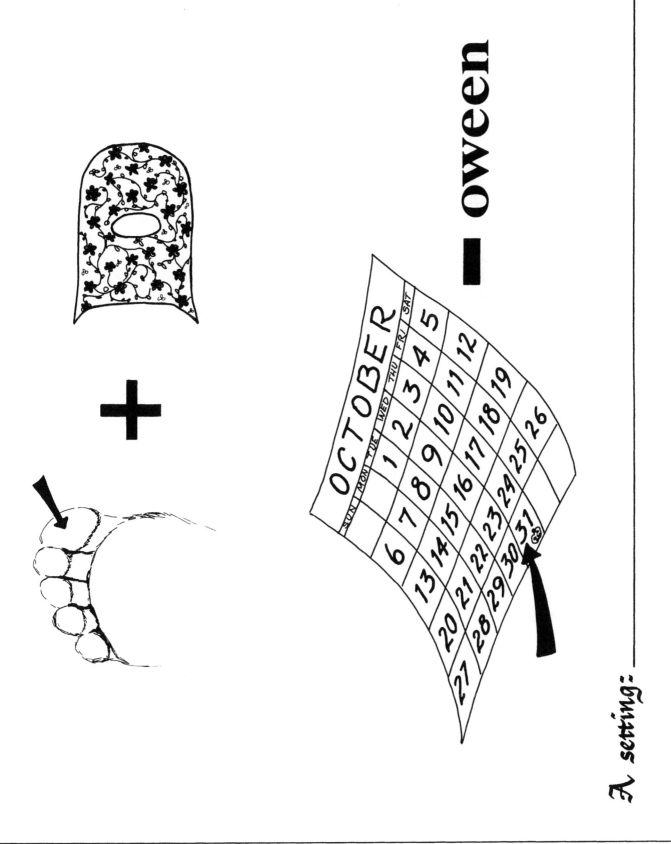

oween

A setting: _____

Rebuses for Readers. 1992. Teacher Ideas Press, a division of Libraries Unlimited • P.O. Box 6633 • Englewood, CO 80155-6633

91

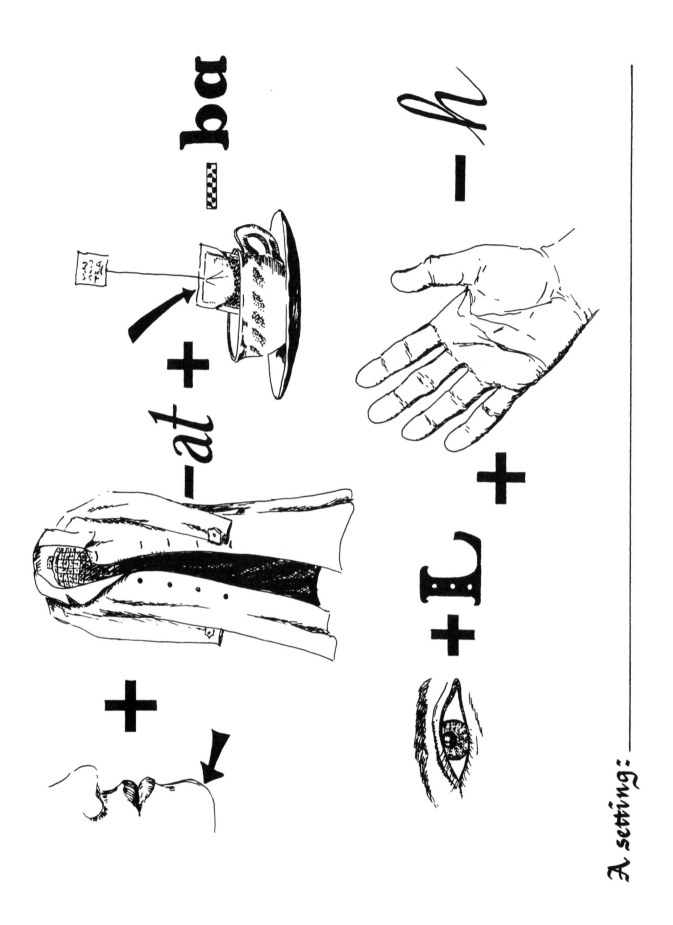

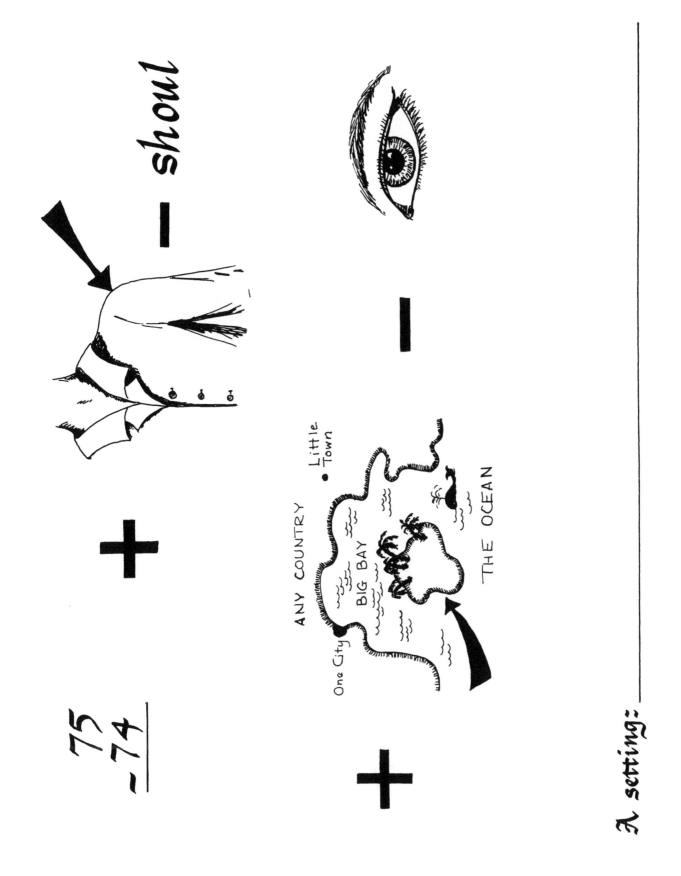

A setting: _____

Rebuses for Readers. 1992. Teacher Ideas Press, a division of Libraries Unlimited • P.O. Box 6633 • Englewood, CO 80155-6633

93

cl, et

6 - l

F +

gl -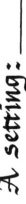

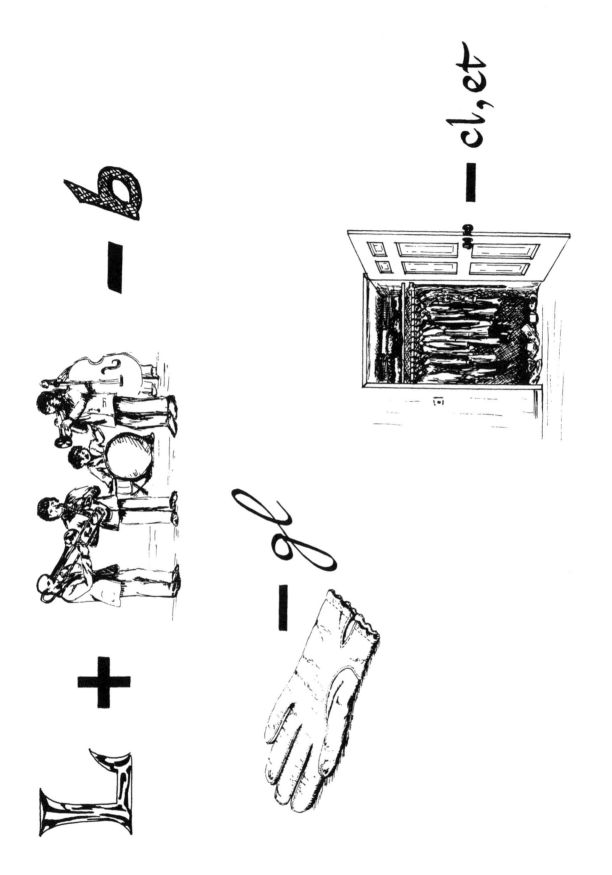

A setting: _____

Rebuses for Readers. 1992. Teacher Ideas Press, a division of Libraries Unlimited • P.O. Box 6633 • Englewood, CO 80155-6633

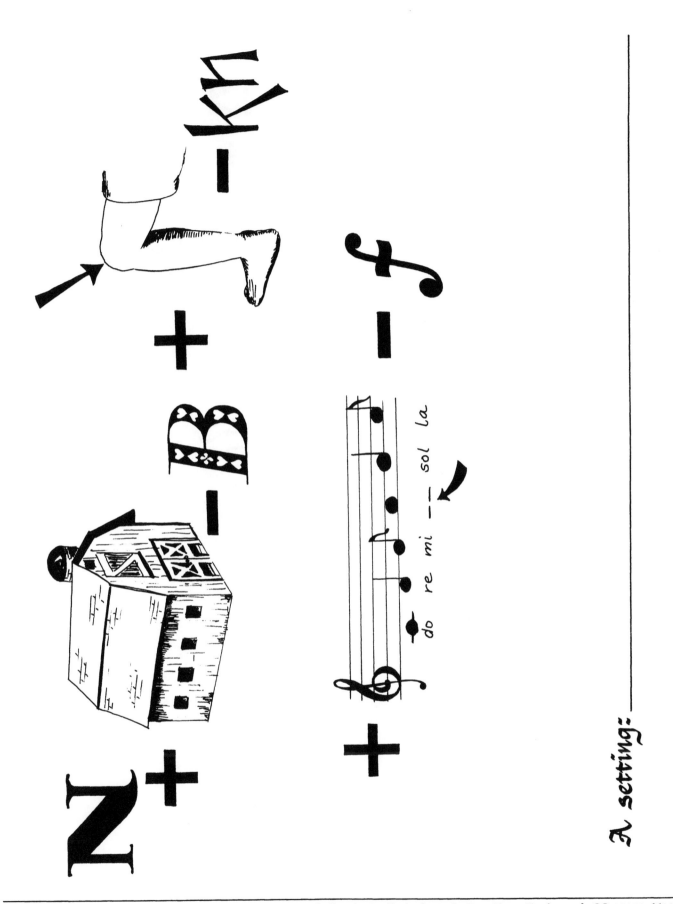

A setting: _____

Rebuses for Readers. 1992. Teacher Ideas Press, a division of Libraries Unlimited • P.O. Box 6633 • Englewood, CO 80155-6633

95

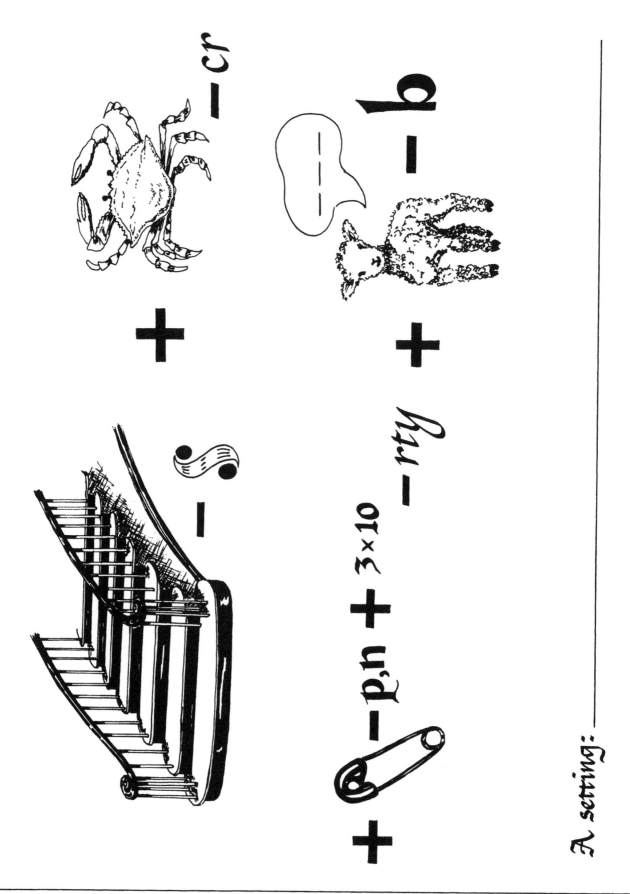

A setting: _____

Rebuses for Readers. 1992. Teacher Ideas Press, a division of Libraries Unlimited • P.O. Box 6633 • Englewood, CO 80155-6633

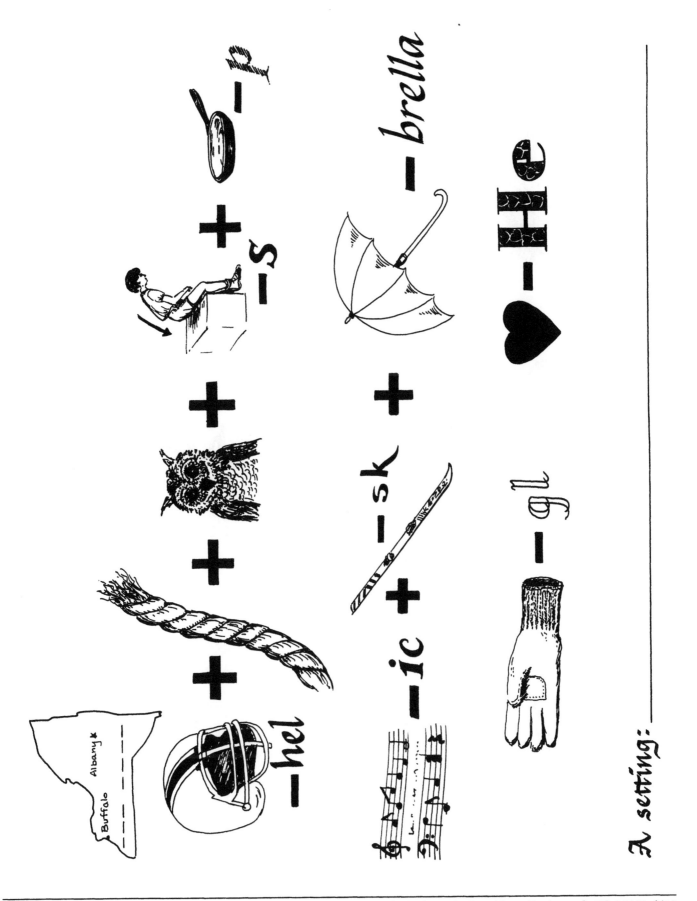

A setting: _____

Rebuses for Readers. 1992. Teacher Ideas Press, a division of Libraries Unlimited • P.O. Box 6633 • Englewood, CO 80155-6633

97

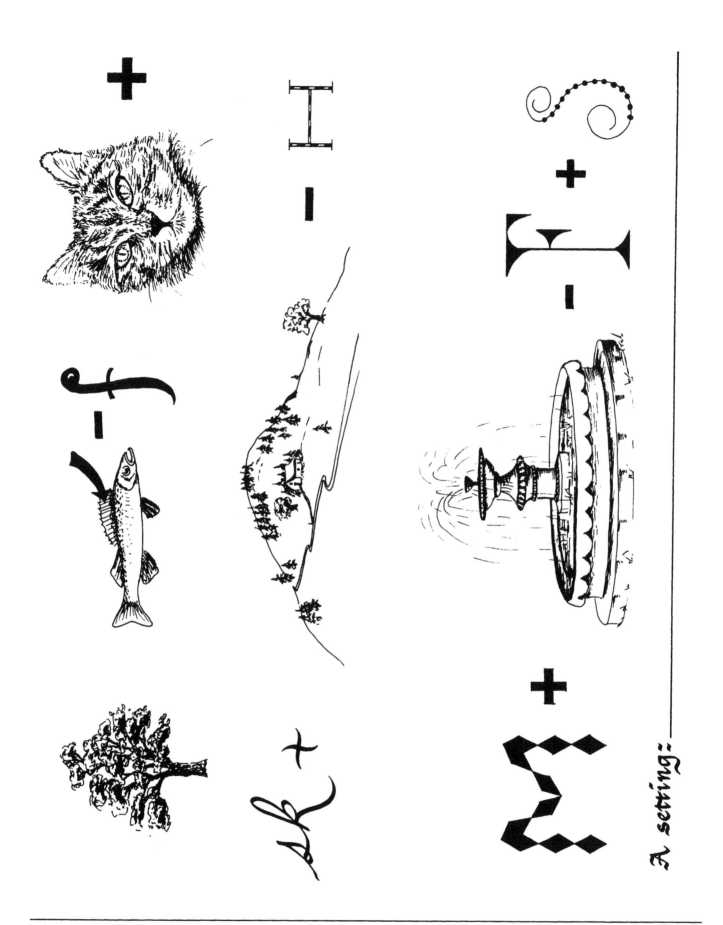

Rebuses for Readers. 1992. Teacher Ideas Press, a division of Libraries Unlimited • P.O. Box 6633 • Englewood, CO 80155-6633

98

5

Ten Make-Your-Own Rebuses and Sample Solutions

Make-Your-Own Rebuses

On pages 100-109 all the pictures for the respective books and authors will work. However, you do not need to use every one. How many rebuses can you make for each page?

Sample Solutions

On pages 110-14 the solutions to these rebuses are not unique. These are examples that show only one of several possible answers for each rebus.

~at	G+	-ℏ	-B	D+	-fr	-L

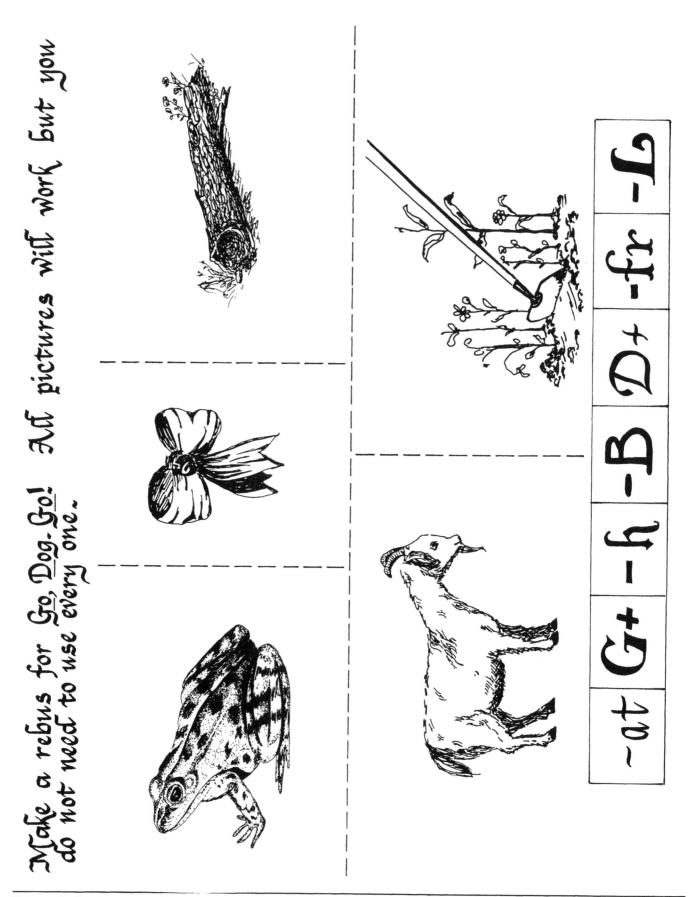

Make a rebus for Go, Dog. Go! All pictures will work but you do not need to use every one.

-at G+ -h -B D+ -fr -L

Rebuses for Readers. 1992. Teacher Ideas Press, a division of Libraries Unlimited • P.O. Box 6633 • Englewood, CO 80155-6633

Make a rebus for Caps for Sale. All pictures will work but you do not need to use every one.

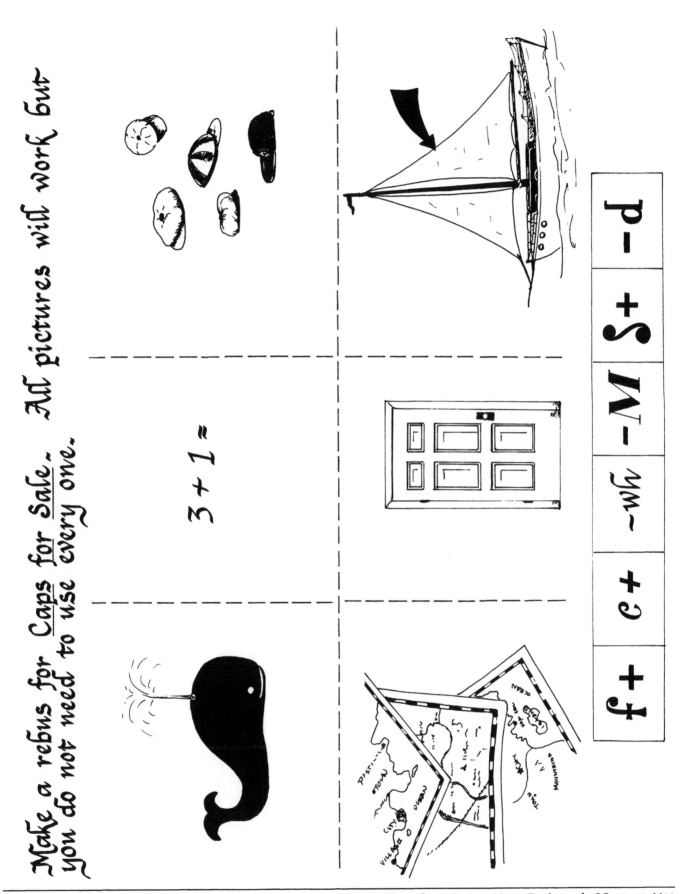

3 + 1 =

| f + | c + | -wh | -w | s + | -p |

Make a rebus for Beatrix Potter. All pictures will work but you do not need to use every one.

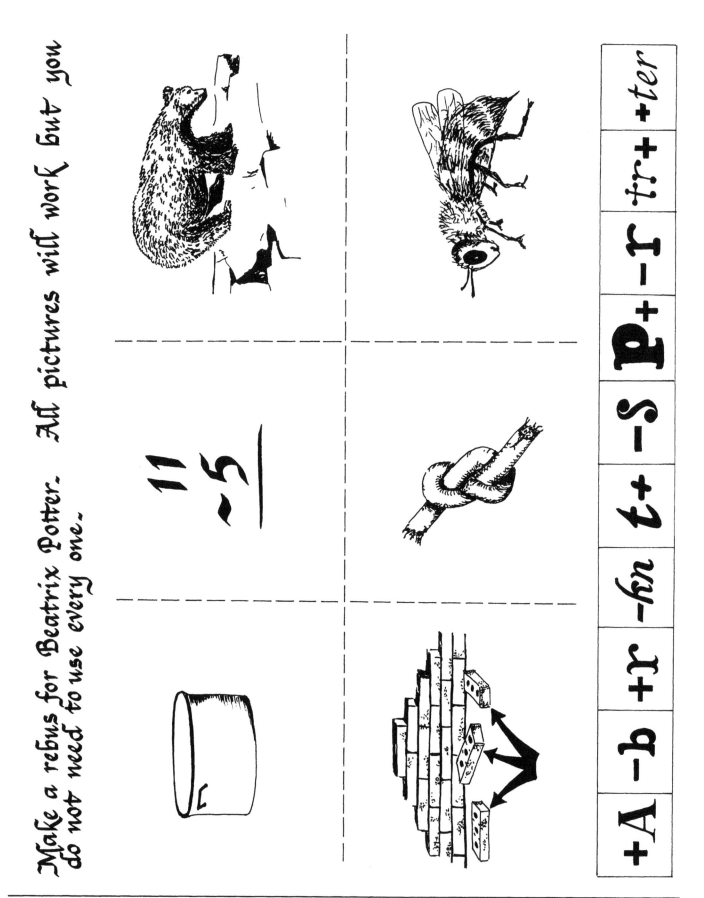

+A	-b	+r	-kn	t+	-S	p+	-r	tr+
								+ter

Rebuses for Readers. 1992. Teacher Ideas Press, a division of Libraries Unlimited • P.O. Box 6633 • Englewood, CO 80155-6633

Make a rebus for Cinderella. All pictures will work but you do not need to use every one.

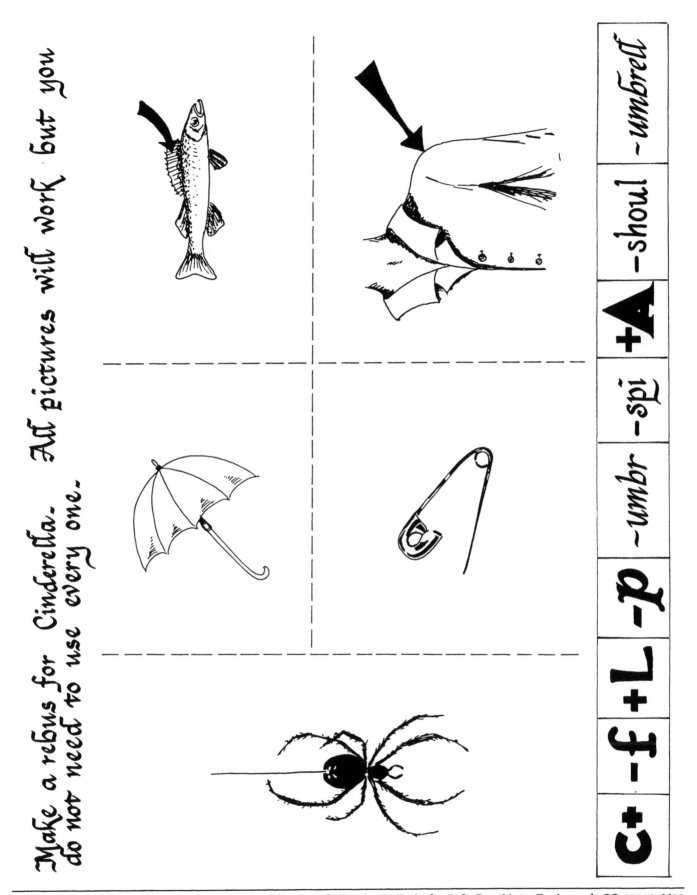

C+	-f	+L	-p	-umbr	-spi	+A	-shoul	-umbrell

Rebuses for Readers. 1992. Teacher Ideas Press, a division of Libraries Unlimited • P.O. Box 6633 • Englewood, CO 80155-6633

Make a rebus for Winnie-the-Pooh. All pictures will work but you do not need to use every one.

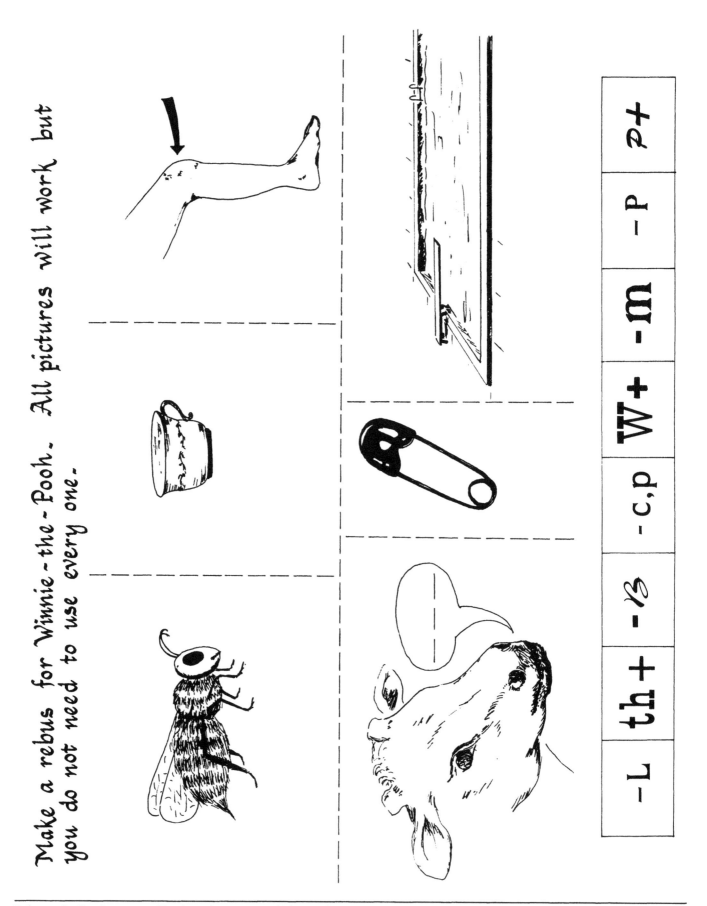

-L	th+	-ß	-c,p	W+	-m	-P	P+

Rebuses for Readers. 1992. Teacher Ideas Press, a division of Libraries Unlimited • P.O. Box 6633 • Englewood, CO 80155-6633

Make a rebus for *The Brothers Grimm.* All pictures will work but you do not need to use every one.

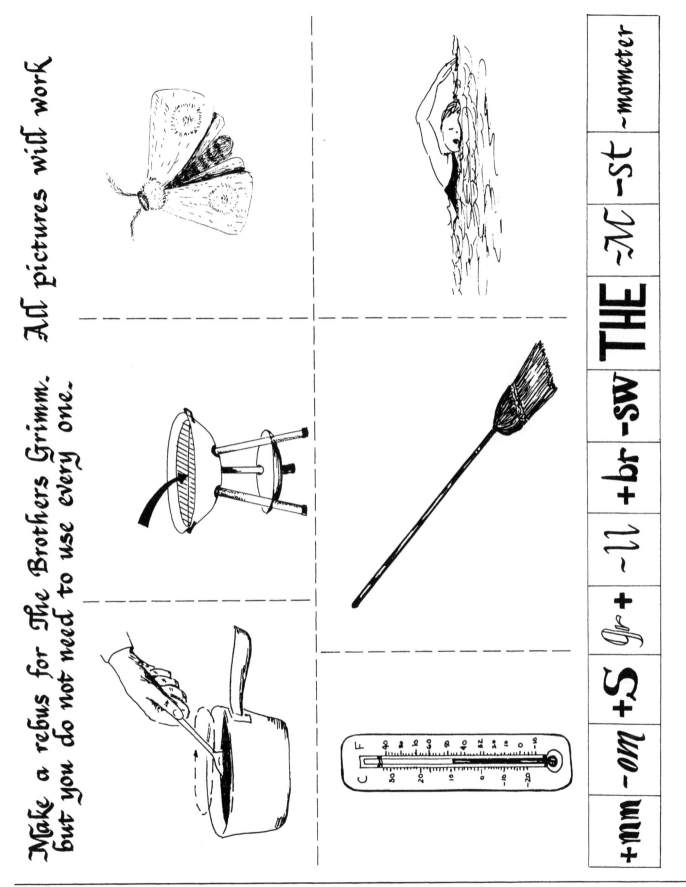

+mm ~om	+S	gr+ ~ll	+br ~sw	THE	~n ~st	~mometer

Rebuses for Readers. 1992. Teacher Ideas Press, a division of Libraries Unlimited • P.O. Box 6633 • Englewood, CO 80155-6633

105

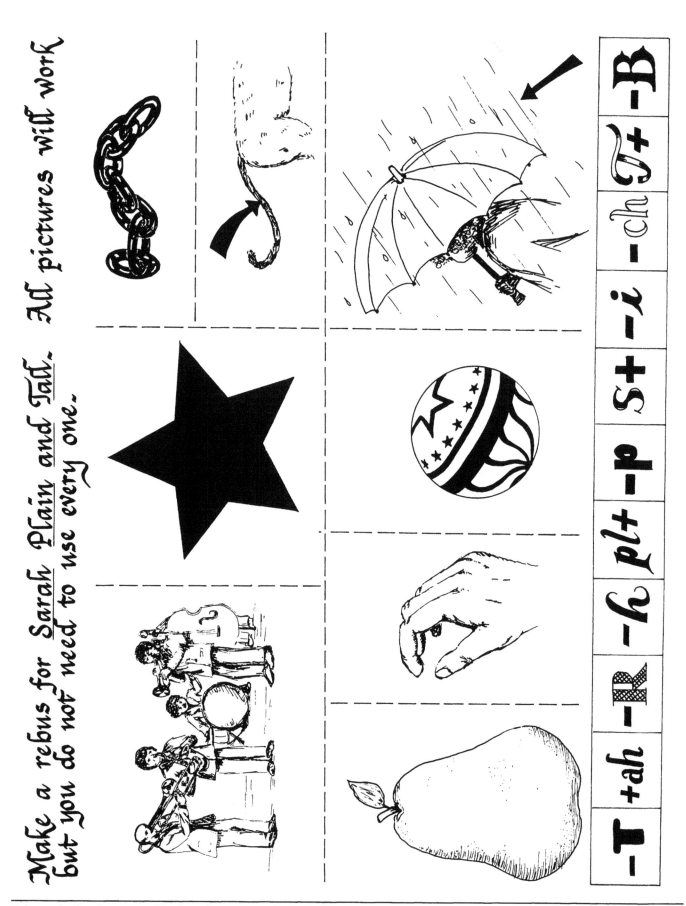

Make a rebus for *Sarah Plain and Tall*. All pictures will work but you do not need to use every one.

-T +ah	-R	-h	pl+ p	S+ -i	-ch	T+	-B

Rebuses for Readers. 1992. Teacher Ideas Press, a division of Libraries Unlimited • P.O. Box 6633 • Englewood, CO 80155-6633

Make a rebus for Plum Creek. All pictures will work but you do not need to use every one.

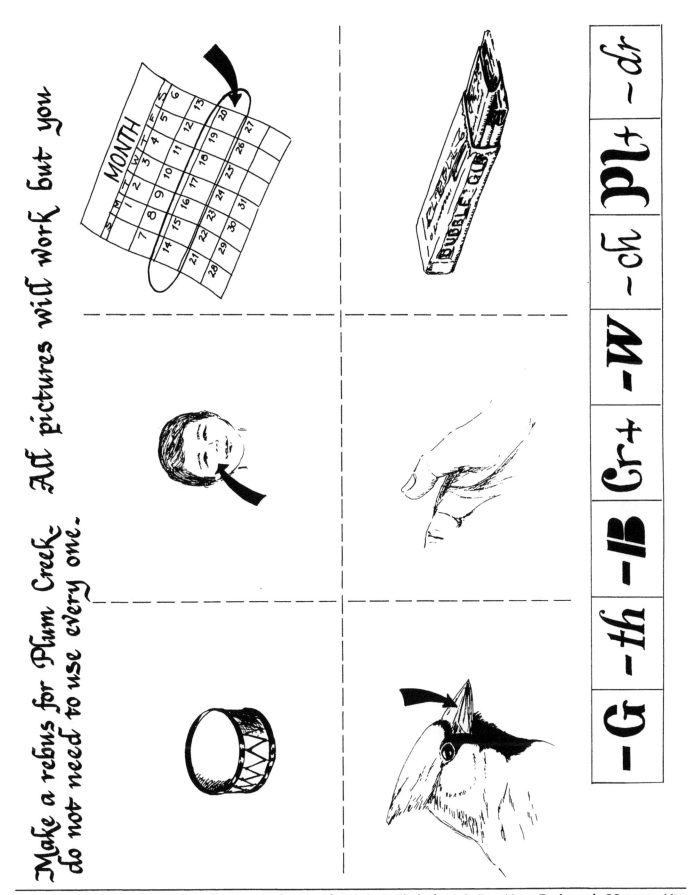

-G	-th	-B	Cr+	-W	-ch	pl+	-dr

Rebuses for Readers. 1992. Teacher Ideas Press, a division of Libraries Unlimited • P.O. Box 6633 • Englewood, CO 80155-6633

Make a rebus for The Westing Game. All pictures will work but you do not need to use every one.

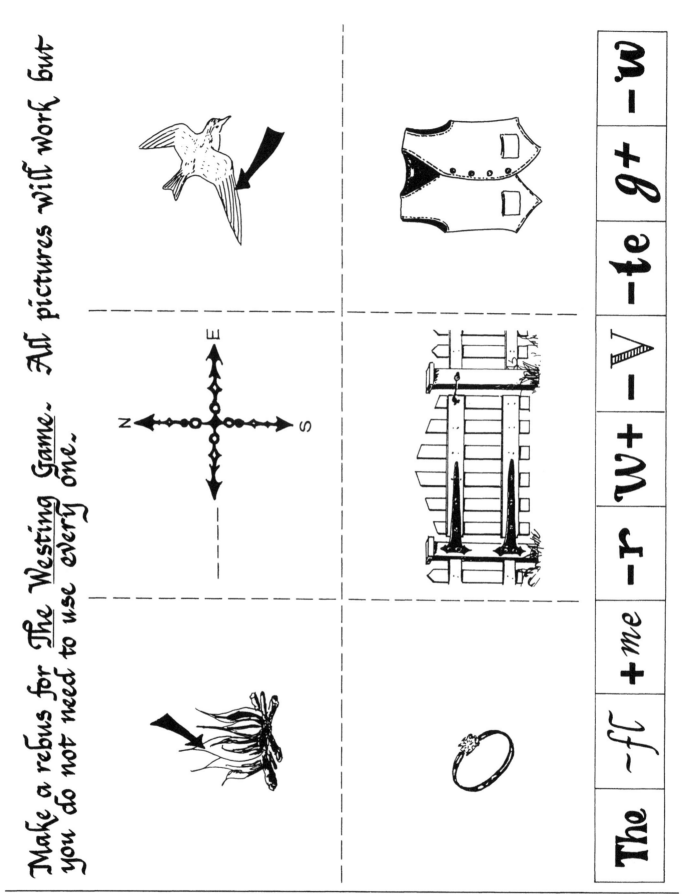

| The | -ff | +me | -r | W+ | -V | -te | g+ | -w |

Rebuses for Readers. 1992. Teacher Ideas Press, a division of Libraries Unlimited • P.O. Box 6633 • Englewood, CO 80155-6633

108

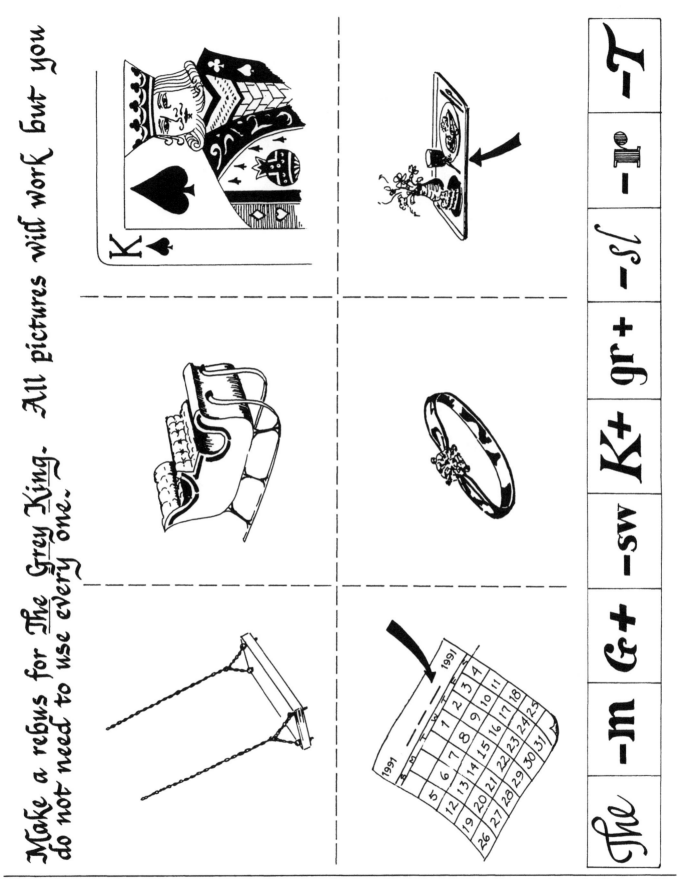

Make a rebus for <u>The</u> <u>Grey</u> <u>King</u>. All pictures will work but you do not need to use every one.

Rebuses for Readers. 1992. Teacher Ideas Press, a division of Libraries Unlimited • P.O. Box 6633 • Englewood, CO 80155-6633

109

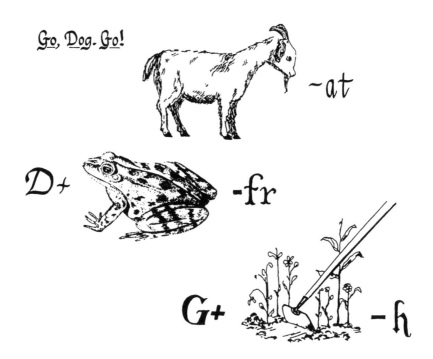

Go, Dog. Go!

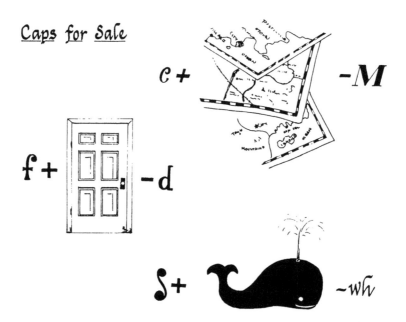

Caps for Sale

Rebuses for Readers. 1992. Teacher Ideas Press, a division of Libraries Unlimited • P.O. Box 6633 • Englewood, CO 80155-6633

110

+ A + tr + $\dfrac{11}{5}$ − S

P + − kn + ter

Cinderella

c + − f +

− spi + − umbr

Rebuses for Readers. 1992. Teacher Ideas Press, a division of Libraries Unlimited • P.O. Box 6633 • Englewood, CO 80155-6633

Winnie-the-Pooh

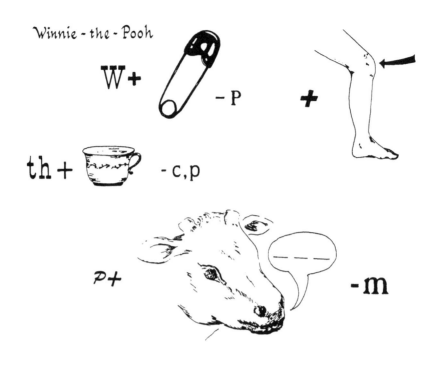

W + [safety pin] - P   [leg] +

th + [cup] - c,p

P + [cow with speech bubble] - m

The Brothers Grimm

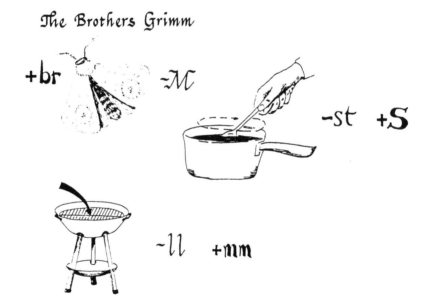

+br [bee] -M   [pan/hand] -st +S

[grill] -ll +mm

Rebuses for Readers. 1992. Teacher Ideas Press, a division of Libraries Unlimited • P.O. Box 6633 • Englewood, CO 80155-6633

<u>Sarah</u> <u>Plain</u> <u>and</u> <u>Tall</u>

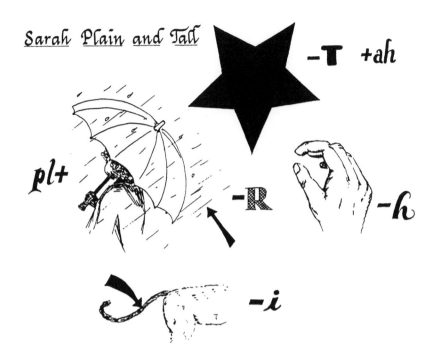

pl+ ... ★ -T +ah ... -R ... -h ... -i

Plum Creek

Pl+ ... -G

Cr+ ... -ch

Rebuses for Readers. 1992. Teacher Ideas Press, a division of Libraries Unlimited • P.O. Box 6633 • Englewood, CO 80155-6633

The Westing Game.

The

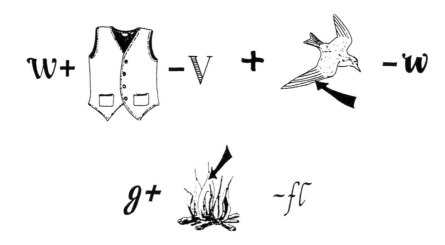

$W+$ 🦺 $-V$ $+$ 🐦 $-W$

$g+$ 🔥 $-fl$

The Grey King

The

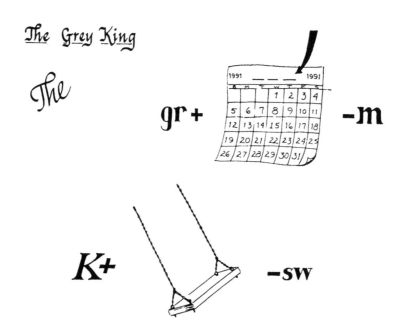

$gr+$ 📅 $-m$

$K+$ 🪆 $-sw$

Rebuses for Readers. 1992. Teacher Ideas Press, a division of Libraries Unlimited • P.O. Box 6633 • Englewood, CO 80155-6633

114

CHAPTER
6
Challenges

To the Student:

Use the pictures on the following pages to make your own rebuses. You have to add and subtract the appropriate letters, and you need to put in plus and minus signs. You may want to make up math problems for parts of the rebus, draw simple shapes such as arrows or squares, and use maps from an atlas. If an animal is pictured, you could put in a word balloon above its head to refer to the sound the animal makes. If an animal has a word balloon above its head in the picture, cut it off if you want to use the name of the animal. Use arrows to point to particular parts of a picture (for example, the string of the balloon). Add to this supply of drawings pictures you cut from magazines. For even more fun, draw your own pictures.

By thinking hard, you should be able to put almost anything into rebus form. You could choose a famous quote, a funny passage from a book, a common saying, or a title of a favorite book. You could even use a short story or a poem and translate a few of the words into pictures as shown in the nursery rhyme, *Little Jack Horner*.

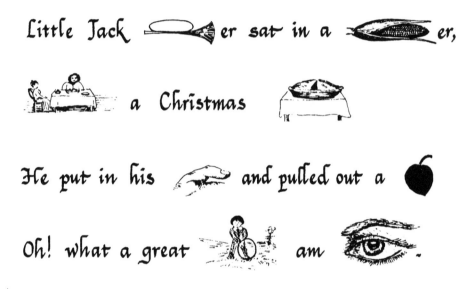

Fig. 1. Rebus based on verse from *Mother Goose in Hieroglyphics*. (Courtesy of the Lilly Library, Indiana University, Bloomington, Indiana.)

Here are some very challenging book titles for you to try to put into rebus form:

1. *Alexander and the Terrible, Horrible, No Good, Very Bad Day* (Judith Viorst)

2. *From the Mixed-Up Files of Mrs. Basil E. Frankweiler* (E. L. Konigsburg)

3. *And to Think That I Saw It on Mulberry Street* (Dr. Seuss)

4. *The 500 Hats of Bartholomew Cubbins* (Dr. Seuss)

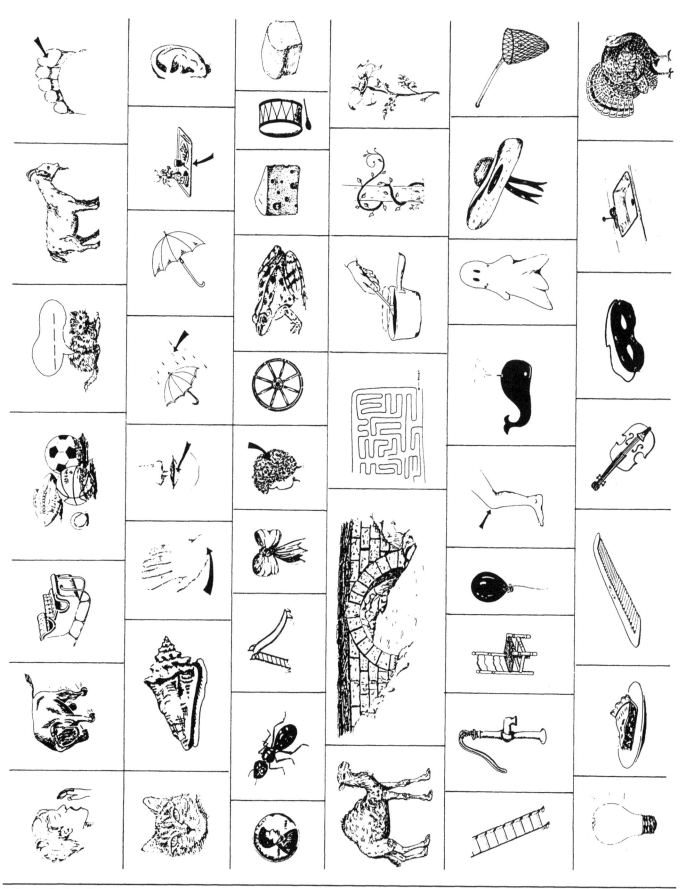

Rebuses for Readers. 1992. Teacher Ideas Press, a division of Libraries Unlimited • P.O. Box 6633 • Englewood, CO 80155-6633

116

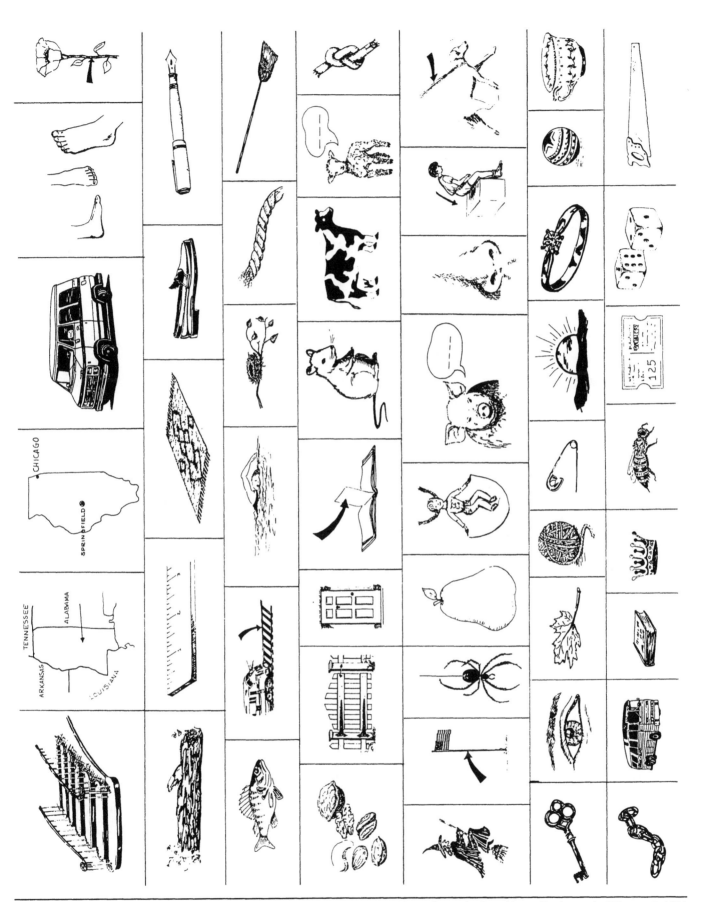

Rebuses for Readers. 1992. Teacher Ideas Press, a division of Libraries Unlimited • P.O. Box 6633 • Englewood, CO 80155-6633

117

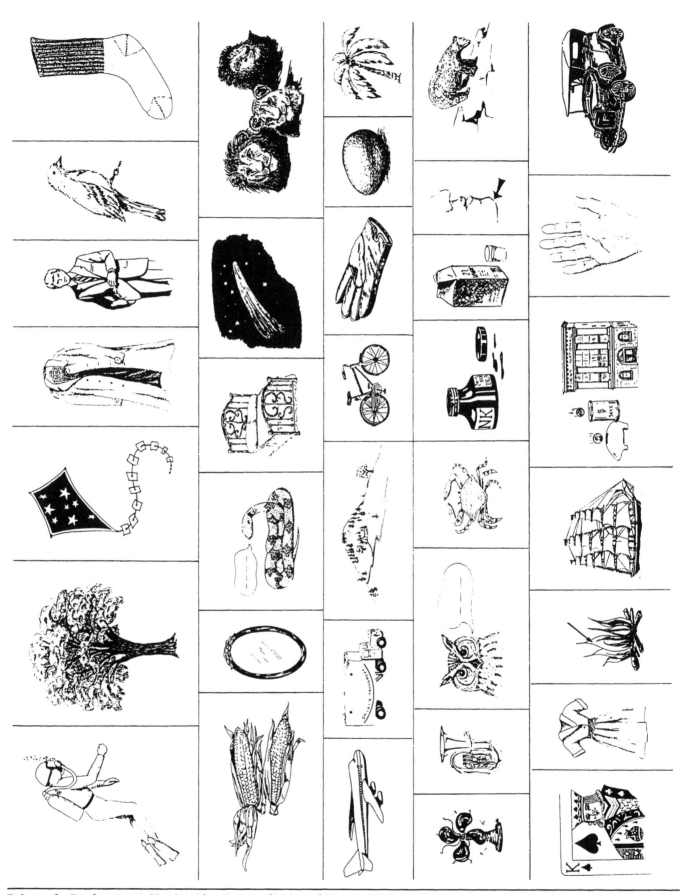

Rebuses for Readers. 1992. Teacher Ideas Press, a division of Libraries Unlimited • P.O. Box 6633 • Englewood, CO 80155-6633

118

Bibliography

Alcott, Louisa May
5-8

Little Women. Several editions, 1868
Family stories

This timeless classic tells of the four March sisters growing up during the Civil War and of the struggle of headstrong, self-centered Jo as she attempts to tame her rebellious personality.

Allard, Harry
1-3

Miss Nelson Is Missing. Boston: Houghton Mifflin, 1978
School stories

Sweet Miss Nelson has the worst behaved class in the school. One day a substitute teacher, witchy Viola Swamp, appears. She is determined to whip the naughty children into shape, and she succeeds.

Andersen, Hans Christian
1-6

Several editions
Fairy tales

Various fairy tales.

Armstrong, William
5-7

Sounder. New York: Harper & Row, 1969
African Americans

A poverty-stricken Black family lives in the South during the Depression. When the father steals food to feed his hungry children, he is imprisoned. This is a story of the courage of a boy and a dog.

Atwater, Florence and Richard
3-5

Mr. Popper's Penguins. Boston: Little, Brown, 1938
Funny stories

This mild-mannered house painter with an interest in polar exploration finds his life is changed when he receives a penguin as a gift. One penguin leads to another, and soon he is in show business.

Banks, Lynn Reid.
4-7

The Indian in the Cupboard. New York: Doubleday, 1985
Fantasy

Omri begins an incredible adventure when he discovers that when a magic key is turned in the lock of an old cupboard, the tiny plastic Indian he put inside comes to life!

Barrie, Sir James
5-6

Peter Pan. Several editions, 1911
Fantasy

Peter can fly and he never grows up! Wendy, John, and Michael fly with him to Never-Land where they have adventures with pirates, the fairy Tinker Bell, and the Lost Boys.

Baum, L. Frank
3-6

The Wizard of Oz. Several editions, 1900
Fantasy

Dorothy and her dog Toto are carried by a cyclone from Kansas to the land of the Munchkins where she begins a wonderful adventure in the Land of Oz. She travels with the Cowardly Lion, the Scarecrow, and the Tin Woodman, and they are all pursued by the Wicked Witch.

Berenstain, Jan and Stan Berenstain
1-2

Berenstain Bears series. New York: Random House, 1966
Funny stories

Nonsense stories in which a human-like bear family goes from one hilarious adventure to another.

Blos, Joan
5-8

A Gathering of Days: A New England Girl's Journal, 1830-1832. New York: Scribner, 1979
Historical fiction

Catherine Hall begins a diary of her 14th year growing up in New Hampshire in 1830. Her mother is dead and her father is about to remarry. Catherine must grow and adjust to change, loss, and saying "good-bye."

Blume, Judy
3-6

Tales of a Fourth Grade Nothing. New York: Dutton, 1972
Funny stories

Nine-year-old Peter puts up with an awful lot of trouble caused by his two-year-old brother, Fudge, who monopolizes the family's attention. But when his pet turtle is missing, Peter's patience comes to an end!

Burnett, Frances Hodgson
5-6

The Secret Garden. Several editions, 1909
Adventure

Mary is orphaned when her parents die of cholera in India. She is sent to live with her uncle, a hunchbacked recluse, in his huge old house on the Englisn moors. One night Mary hears a child crying, so she investigates. So begins the mystery and adventure.

Burnford, Sheila
5-7

The Incredible Journey. Boston: Little, Brown, 1971
Animal stories

An old bull terrier, a young Labrador retriever, and a Siamese cat brave hunger, storms, dangerous river crossings, and fights as they travel 250 miles through the Canadian wilderness to reach home.

Byars, Betsy
5-7

Cracker Jackson. New York: Viking, 1985
Friendship

Sweet and pretty Alma used to be Cracker's baby sitter and he stills feels close to her. When he begins to suspect that she is being beaten by her husband, he wants to help, but she says he must keep away.

_____.
5-6

The Not-Just-Anybody Family. New York: Delacorte, 1986
Family stories

When Pap lands in jail, Maggie and Vern decide they must break in to be with him. They don't expect much help from Junior, who is in the hospital after he fell attempting to fly off the barn roof using homemade wings, or from Mom, who is riding on the rodeo circuit.

Carroll, Lewis
5-7

Alice's Adventures in Wonderland. Several editions, 1865
Fantasy

Follow Alice down the rabbit hole and into a magic land where nonsense is the rule. The Mad Hatter, the Doormouse, and the Rabbit are a few of the amazing individuals Alice meets in her wandering.

Cleary, Beverly 3-5	*Henry Huggins*. New York: Morrow, 1950 Funny stories Henry is a typical boy who innocently gets himself into all sorts of problems. He picks up a stray dog and sets out for adventure. Their exploits include collecting over a thousand worms and breeding hundreds of guppies.
_____. 3-5	*Ramona the Pest*. New York: Morrow, 1968 School stories Ramona has started kindergarten, and her good intentions vanish when she just can't stop pulling her classmate's hair. Ramona becomes a "Kindergarten Dropout"; she is sent home until her behavior improves.
_____. 3-5	*Runaway Ralph* (and other titles in this series). New York: Morrow, 1970 Talking animals Dare-devil Ralph, a small mouse, is fed up with his pesky family, so he decides to put on his crash helmet, get on his motorcycle, and run away. Little does he suspect he'll end up in a cage at a boys' camp.
Cooper, Susan 6	*The Grey King*. Orlando, FL: Harcourt Brace Jovanovich, 1975 Fantasy Will Stanton is in Wales recovering from an illness when he meets a strange albino boy and his dog Cafall. Events help Will regain his lost memory and the realization that he is one of the lost Old Ones who must lead in the battle against the dark.
Dahl, Roald 4-6	*The BFG*. New York: Farrar, 1982 Fantasy A small girl and a giant embark on an adventure to rid England of the giants who have been gobbling up hapless citizens.
_____. 3-5	*Charlie and the Chocolate Factory*. New York: Knopf, 1964 Fantasy Poor little Charlie finds a golden ticket in a candy bar and wins a tour of a magical candy factory, and that's just the beginning of this fantastic adventure.
dePaola, Tomie 1-3	*Strega Nona*. New York: Prentice-Hall, 1975 Folk and fairy tales Strega Nona has a magic pasta pot. One day, while she is away, her helper, Big Anthony, decides to treat the town to free pasta. The trouble is that he doesn't know how to turn it off, so he nearly buries the whole town.
Eastman, P. D. 1	*Go, Dog. Go!* New York: Random House, 1961 Funny stories An easy to read, funny story about all kinds of dogs and their silly antics.
Farley, Walter 4-7	*The Black Stallion*. New York: Random House, 1941 Animal stories Alec Ramsey and a wild, black stallion are the only survivors of a shipwreck, and they live for a while on an uninhabited island. After they are rescued Alec is determined to train the horse for racing.

Fitzgerald, John D.
5-7

The Great Brain. New York: Dial, 1967
Historical fiction

In 1896 T. D. Fitzgerald rocks the town of Adenville, Utah, with his wild exploits and ingenious schemes. His hilarious adventures are told by his younger brother with tall-tale exaggeration.

Freeman, Don
1-2

Corduroy. New York: Viking, 1968
Fantasy

Corduroy is a toy bear waiting in a large department store for someone to take him home. A little girl wants him, but her mother notices a button is missing from his overalls. That night he sets out to find a new button but has an adventure instead.

Gag, Wanda
1-2

Millions of Cats. New York: Coward-McCann, 1928
Animal stories

A very old woman and a very old man are overwhelmed when he goes in search of one little kitten and returns with "millions and billions and trillions of cats."

George, Jean
5-7

My Side of the Mountain. New York: Dutton, 1959
Survival

Sam Gribley is fed up with city life and his large family, so he runs away to a spot in the Catskill Mountains that had once belonged to his grandfather. There he attempts to survive on his own in the wilderness, even through a rugged and lonely winter.

Giff, Patricia Reilly
2-4

The Beast in Mrs. Rooney's Room. New York: Delacorte, 1986
School stories

In September Richard "The Beast" Best tries to cope with having been held back in second grade for another year. This is the first in a series of stories about this class and their adventures over the course of a year.

Grahame, Kenneth
4-6

The Wind in the Willows. Several editions, 1908
Talking animals

This is the story of kindly Badger, good-natured Rat, gullible Mole, and comic Toad. Show-off Toad, following one fad after another, is always falling into troublesome situations from which he must be rescued by Badger, Rat, and Mole.

Grimm, Jacob and Wilhelm
Grimm, eds.
1-3

Cinderella. Several editions, 1812
Folk and fairy tales

A beautiful girl is mistreated by her cruel step-mother and two step-sisters. She is befriended by her fairy godmother and wins a handsome prince.

_____.
1-3

Little Red Riding Hood. Several editions, 1812
Folk and fairy tales

A traditional tale of an innocent little girl who falls into the clutches of a wicked wolf.

_____.
1-3

Rumpelstiltskin. Several editions, 1812
Folk and fairy tales

A familiar tale in which a farmer's daughter is put in danger because of her boastful father. Forced to spin straw into gold in order to satisfy the king, she must barter with an evil little man. She cleverly tricks the little man when he comes to collect his part of the bargain.

Hahn, Mary Downing
5-7

Wait Till Helen Comes. New York: Clarion, 1986.
Ghost stories

A thriller in which a ghost child is determined to lure strange little Heather to her doom. In spite of their dislike of their new step-sister, Molly and Michael realize they must try to save Heather from forces they don't understand.

Henry, Marguerite
4-6

Misty of Chincoteague. Chicago: Rand McNally, 1947
Animal stories

Paul and Maureen have their hearts set on owning the wild pony and her colt that have been brought over from Assateague Island on Pony Penning Day.

Howe, Deborah and James Howe
4-6

Bunnicula: A Rabbit Tale of Mystery. New York: Atheneum, 1979
Talking animals

Is the new pet in the Monroe household responsible for vegetables that are drained of their juices overnight? Chester the cat thinks so, especially because the new little rabbit has the teeth and markings of a vampire!

Irving, Washington
5-8

Rip Van Winkle. Several editions, 1820
Fantasy

Lazy, good-for-nothing Rip fell in with evil companions, and as a result went into a sleep that lasted for twenty years. He found that life in his hometown had changed considerably when he awoke.

Johnson, Crocket
1-2

Harold and the Purple Crayon. New York: Harper & Row, 1955
Fantasy

A small boy "draws" himself into an adventure and then back home again.

King-Smith, Dick
4-6

Harry's Mad. New York: Crown, 1984
Adventure

Harry has been named an heir in his great-uncle's will! He dreams of the riches he may inherit but is disappointed to learn he has been given a talking parrot. Soon, however, he learns that his gift is more exciting than anything he could have dreamed.

Konigsburg, E. L.
4-6

From the Mixed-Up Files of Mrs. Basil E. Frankweiler. New York: Atheneum, 1967. Adventure

Claudia decides to run away from home and to take her younger brother Jamie with her. They devise an ingenious plan to hide out at the Metropolitan Museum of Art in New York City and also investigate the mystery surrounding an alleged Michelangelo statue.

L'Engle, Madeleine
5-7

A Wrinkle in Time. New York: Farrar, Straus & Giroux, 1962
Fantasy

Meg's father was lost while engaging in secret work on the tesseract problem. Meg, her little brother, and her friend Calvin travel through time and space to locate the father who is being held prisoner by the evil IT on a forbidding planet.

Lewis, C. S.
4-6

The Lion, the Witch, and the Wardrobe. New York: Macmillan, 1950
Fantasy

Four English children enter a magic land when they walk through the back of a wardrobe closet. In Narnia they meet the mighty lion Aslan and join with him in the struggle to free the wintery kingdom from the awful spell of the evil White Witch.

Lindgren, Astrid
3-5

Pippi Longstocking. New York: Viking, 1950
Funny stories

Nine-year-old Pippi lives alone and does many miraculous things. She is incredibly strong and has an imagination to match. She, her horse, and her monkey make sure that life is never dull for the residents of their town.

Lobel, Arnold
1-2

Frog and Toad Are Friends. New York: Harper & Row, 1971
Talking animals

Five funny adventures of two best friends.

Lowry, Lois
3-7

Number the Stars and other stories. Boston: Houghton Mifflin, 1989
Historical fiction

A brave Danish girl and her family help smuggle Jewish friends out of Denmark during the Nazi occupation of World War II.

MacLachlan, Patricia
4

Sarah, Plain and Tall. New York: Harper & Row, 1985
Historical fiction

The father of two motherless pioneer children advertises in an Eastern newspaper for a wife. The ad is answered by Sarah who agrees to come and visit and perhaps to stay. The children find that Sarah brings love and music along as well as her cat.

McCloskey, Robert
1-2

Blueberries for Sal. New York: Viking, 1948
Animal stories

A little girl and her mother go blueberry picking on a summer day in Maine, but run into a bear cub and its mother who are also eating berries on the same hill.

_____.
4-5

Homer Price. New York: Viking, 1943
Funny stories

Incredible complications arise when Homer and his pet skunk Aroma get involved with bank robbers, a donut machine, and a comic book hero named Super Duper.

_____.
1

Make Way for Ducklings. New York: Viking, 1941
Talking animals

Mr. and Mrs. Mallard set out in search of the perfect place to raise their family of baby ducks. With the help of a policeman they finally settle on the pond at Boston's Public Gardens.

Milne, A. A.
4

Winnie-the-Pooh. New York: Dutton, 1974
Talking animals

Christopher Robin's toy bear named Pooh comes to life in this story filled with adventures and the "hums of Pooh." Other characters who share in the fantastic escapades are Eeyore, Piglet, Kanga, Rabbit, and Roo.

Parish, Peggy
1-2

Amelia Bedelia. New York: Harper & Row, 1963
Funny stories

This silly maid causes funny things to happen when she follows all instructions to the letter.

Paterson, Katherine
4-6

Bridge to Terabithia. New York: Crowell, 1977
Friendship

Fifth-grader Jess at first avoids his new neighbor Leslie because she is very different from the other girls in his rural Virginia school. When a strong friendship develops, they build a secret kingdom in the woods where Leslie brings Jess new experiences including grief when she dies.

Peck, Robert Newton
4-6

Soup and Me. New York: Knopf, 1975
Friendship

In rural Vermont, during the 1920s, Soup and Rob get involved in hilarious adventures like stealing the town's largest pumpkin and ringing the courthouse bell.

Peet, Bill
1-4

Various titles.
Talking animals

Pinkwater, Daniel
3-5

Various titles.
Funny stories

Potter, Beatrix
1-3

Tale of Peter Rabbit and other stories. New York: Warne, 1903
Talking animals

A naughty rabbit learns why his mother warned him never to go into Mr. McGregor's garden.

Raskin, Ellen
5

The Westing Game. New York: Dutton, 1978
Mystery

An eccentric millionaire has died and in order to claim his fortune his heirs must solve clues to an ingenious puzzle. A "murder" and shifting identities are only two of the twists in the plot that make this an exciting mystery.

Rawls, Wilson
5-8

Where the Red Fern Grows. New York: Doubleday, 1961
Animal stories

A young boy, growing up in the Ozark Mountains, works to earn the money for two hunting dogs. He strives to train them as championship coon hounds and then to win the gold cup.

Rey, H. A.
1-2

Curious George. Boston: Houghton Mifflin, 1941
Funny stories

This favorite picture book tells of the adventures of a small monkey helped by his friend, the Man in the Yellow Hat, as he adjusts to city life.

Roberts, Willo Davis
4-7

The View from the Cherry Tree. New York: Atheneum, 1975
Mysteries

Rob is a horrified witness to a murder, but no one in his busy household will listen to him when he tries to tell his story. While they are all involved with preparations for his sister's wedding, Rob begins to realize that he is the new target of the murderer.

Robinson, Barbara
4-6

The Best Christmas Pageant Ever. New York: Harper & Row, 1972
Funny stories

Everyone in town predicts disaster when the horrible Herdman children decide to star in the Sunday school Christmas program.

Rockwell, Thomas
3-6

How to Eat Fried Worms. New York: Franklin Watts, 1973
Funny stories

Billy will do almost anything to earn the $50 he needs for a used minibike. Will he even eat a worm a day for 15 days? Alan bets he won't, but he'll give him the $50 if he does. Everyone pitches in to help when Billy agrees to try.

Selden, George
3-6

The Cricket in Times Square. New York: Farrar, Straus & Giroux, 1960
Talking animals

Chester, a musical country cricket, suddenly finds himself lost in the Times Square subway station. He is befriended by a mouse, a cat, and a boy who teach him about city life. He earns fame when his wonderful musical talent is discovered and enjoyed by busy commuters.

Sendak, Maurice
1-2

Chicken Soup with Rice. New York: Harper & Row, 1962
Funny stories

A book that illustrates interesting and hilarious ways of enjoying chicken soup during all months and seasons of the year.

———.
1-2

Where the Wild Things Are. New York: Harper & Row, 1963
Fantasy

When Max puts on his wolf suit he behaves like a wild thing, so he is sent to bed without his supper. He dreams of a trip to a fantasy island where he rules the monsters and joins them in a real rumpus.

Seuss, Dr.
1-3

And to Think That I Saw It on Mulberry Street. New York: Random House, 1937
Fantasy

Marvelous things occur in the imagination of this boy on the way home from school. A plain horse and cart even grow into a circus bandwagon drawn by an elephant and two giraffes.

———.
1-3

The 500 Hats of Bartholomew Cubbins. New York: Random House, 1938
Funny stories

Every time a boy takes off his hat to honor the king, a new one appears making the king very angry.

———.
1-3

Horton Hatches the Egg. New York: Random House, 1940
Funny stories

Horton, a good-natured elephant, unwittingly becomes a long-term baby sitter for a bird's egg while the mother flies off on a vacation.

Silverstein, Shel
2-6

Where the Sidewalk Ends. New York: Harper & Row, 1974
Poetry

A collection of 127 hilarious poems to be enjoyed by all.

Slobodkina, Esphyr
1

Caps for Sale. New York: Harper Collins, 1947
Funny stories

Monkeys steal a peddler's caps while he naps under a tree, but they give them back following the adage, "Monkey see, monkey do."

Sobol, Donald
3-5

Encyclopedia Brown. New York: Lodestar, 1963
Mysteries

Even though the chief of police in Idaville can't solve the mysteries in this book, they are easily explained by his brilliant son. Readers have a chance to test their sleuthing ability, too.

Taylor, Mildred
5-7

Roll of Thunder, Hear My Cry. New York: Dial, 1976
African-Americans

Life in the South during the Depression was hard for all families but especially for Black people. Cassie and her family struggle against bigotry and exploitation with dignity, courage, and pride.

Travers, P. L.
4-6

Mary Poppins. Orlando, FL: Harcourt Brace Jovanovich, 1981
Fantasy

Mary, an uncommon nursemaid, takes her charges, Jane and Michael Banks, on funny and magical adventures.

Twain, Mark
6 +

Tom Sawyer and other stories. Several editions, 1876
Adventure

Van Allsburg, Chris
1-5

Jumanji. Boston: Houghton Mifflin, 1981
Fantasy

A brother and sister find a game left in a park. They experiment with it. To their horror each roll of the dice brings a new hazard and they must play the game to completion.

———.
1-5

The Polar Express. Boston: Houghton Mifflin, 1985
Fantasy

A boy goes on a thrilling Christmas Eve train ride to the North Pole where he meets Santa Claus and receives the first gift of Christmas.

Viorst, Judith
1-3

Alexander and the Terrible, Horrible, No Good, Very Bad Day. New York: Atheneum, 1972. Funny Stories

Everything goes wrong for Alexander from the time he gets up in the morning with gum in his hair, until he goes to bed at night in his hated railroad train pajamas. Will he move to Australia as he threatens?

Voigt, Cynthia
5-8

Homecoming. New York: Atheneum, 1981
Family stories

When the four Tillerman children are abandoned by their mother outside a shopping mall, they set out on foot to find a relative they've never met. Their journey takes them over many miles and into a series of adventures that are realistic and sometimes frightening.

Warner, Gertrude
2-5

The Boxcar Children. Niles, IL: Whitman, 1950
Adventure

Four children run away from an orphanage when they fear their grandfather, whom they've never met will come for them. They manage to fend for themselves by living in an abandoned boxcar.

White, E. B.
3-6

Charlotte's Web. New York: Harper & Row, 1952
Talking animals

Wilbur, the pig, turns to his friend Charlotte, the spider, when he learns he is to be killed. Charlotte devises an ingenious scheme to save her friend.

Wilder, Laura Ingalls
3-5

Little House on the Prairie. New York: Harper & Row, 1953
Historical fiction

Here is the famous story of the journey made by Ma, Pa, Mary, and Laura to their new home in the Indian territory.

———.
5

On the Banks of Plum Creek. New York: Harper & Row, 1953
Historical fiction

Laura and her family move to Minnesota, and for a while, they live in a dugout home. This story is filled with adventure as the Ingalls face a plague of grasshoppers, a blizzard, and a prairie fire, and Laura must endure Nellie Olson.

Author/Title Rebus
Locator Index

R following a page number indicates a rebus puzzle for author, book title, character, or setting.

Genre Rebus Locator Index

R following a page number indicates a rebus puzzle for author, book title, character, or setting.

Historical Fiction

Mysteries

Poetry

School Stories

Survival

Talking Animals

Grade/Level Rebus
Locator Index

R following a page number indicates a rebus puzzle for author, title, character, or setting.

135

4-7	Farley, Walter	*The Black Stallion*, 1, 4, 42R, 121
	Banks, Lynn Reid	*The Indian in the Cupboard*, 1, 3, 30R, 55, 68R, 72, 86R, 119
5	Raskin, Ellen	*The Westing Game*, 99, 108R, 125
	Roberts, Willo Davis	*The View from the Cherry Tree*, 1, 4, 40R, 125
	Wilder, Laura Ingalls	*On the Banks of Plum Creek*, 55, 67R, 72, 81R, 99, 107R, 128
5-6	Barrie, Sir James	*Peter Pan*, 88, 90R, 119
	Burnett, Frances Hodgson	*The Secret Garden*, 1, 4, 51R, 120
	Byars, Betsy	*The Not-Just-Anybody Family*, 1, 3, 35R, 55, 69R, 120
5-7	Armstrong, William	*Sounder*, 1, 3, 38R, 119
	Burnford, Sheila	*The Incredible Journey*, 1, 4, 47R, 120
	Byars, Betsy	*Cracker Jackson*, 1, 4, 43R, 55, 69R, 120
	Carroll, Lewis	*Alice's Adventures in Wonderland*, 88, 93R, 120
	Fitzgerald, John D.	*The Great Brain*, 1, 4, 45R, 122
	George, Jean	*My Side of the Mountain*, 88, 98R, 122
	Hahn, Mary Downing	*Wait Till Helen Comes*, 1, 4, 52R, 123
	L'Engle, Madeleine	*A Wrinkle in Time*, 1, 4, 54R, 72, 85R, 123
	Taylor, Mildred	*Roll of Thunder, Hear My Cry*, 1. 4, 50R, 127
5-8	Alcott, Louisa May	*Little Women*, 1, 4, 48R, 72, 84R, 119
	Blos, Joan	*A Gathering of Days: A New England Girl's Journal, 1830-32*, 1, 4, 44R, 120
	Irving, Washington	*Rip Van Winkle*, 1, 4, 49R, 123
	Rawls, Wilson	*Where the Red Fern Grows*, 1, 4, 53R, 125
	Voigt, Cynthia	*Homecoming*, 1, 4, 46R, 72, 87R, 127
6-8	Cooper, Susan	*The Grey King*, 99, 109R, 121

About the Authors

Pat Martin, Joanne Kelly, and Kay Grabow have collaborated together for over 20 years daring children to discover that reading is fun! They have shared their interests in literature, art, and puzzles with their own families and with two generations of children at the Thomas Paine Elementary School in Urbana, Illinois. Joanne Kelly is the school librarian and Kay Grabow is a fourth grade teacher. Pat Martin, an art coordinator by profession, has contributed hundreds of hours as a school library volunteer. They consider the children to be their greatest challenge and their never-ending source of inspiration.

Pat Martin (left), Joanne Kelly (center), and Kay Grabow (right)